Twentysomething, Floundering, and Off the Yuppie Track

Twentysomething, Floundering, and Off the Yuppie Track

A self-help guide to making it through your twenties

STEVEN GIBB

THE NOBLE PRESS, INC.

CHICAGO

Printed in the United States of America

Library of Congress Cataloging-in-Publication Data

Gibb, Steven, 1964–
    Twentysomething, floundering, and off the yuppie track : a self-
help guide to making it through your twenties / Steven Gibb.
        p.   cm.
    ISBN 1-879360-03-9 (pbk.) : $10.95
    1. Young adults — United States — Life skills guides.   I. Title.
HQt99.7.G55   1992
305.23'5 — dc20   91-50625
                                                                     CIP

Noble Press books are available in bulk at discount prices.
Single copies are available prepaid direct from the publisher.

The Noble Press, Inc.
213 W. Institute Place, Suite 508
Chicago, Illinois 60610
(800) 486–7737

TABLE OF CONTENTS

For my parents
Bruce Lorenzo and Sara Lovett Gibb

Acknowledgements

I FEEL fortunate to count many of the people who helped put this book together as friends. I would first like to thank everyone who spoke with me about the project in the last three years, especially the extended family and the Sunday brunch crowd. Without their responsiveness and encouragement this book would not have been written.

Thanks to Chris Sulavik, Judith Jones and her family, Terry Dunivin, the Chippewa Blood brothers, Stephen Segar, Mary Kay Magistad, Natalie, Scott, Chuck, and Ken Cunningham, Carolyn Vogel, Ami Walsh, Derrick Widmarck, and the Dean of Students Office at Purdue University.

I would also like to recognize the contributions made by my professors in the Marriage and Family Therapy program at Purdue University: Drs. Sprenkle, Piercy, Nelson, and Figley. I owe gratitude to the staff at the University of Michigan's Center for Human Growth and Development for sharing their views, and especially to Dr. Fred Bookstein, who provided a thoroughgoing critique of the early version of the manuscript.

Joseph Curtin deserves special mention for seeing this project through from beginning to end and straightening me out on several key issues. In playing Devil's Advocate he sometimes made me wonder if he had become the devil himself, but this book wouldn't have been the same without him. Lastly, I am indebted to my editors, Suzanne Roe, Mark Harris, and Douglas Seibold of Noble Press, for expertly guiding me through the various phases of book building.

Introduction

THE FUTURE looks bright when you turn twenty. And why not? As a sophomore in college, you only have to write a few papers and cram for exams to justify your existence. You're surrounded by hundreds of charming, single people of the opposite sex; there are Friday night keggers, Spring formals, road trips, summer vacation. Ahhhh yes.

As long as you're in the dorm, you don't have to shop for food, cook, or clean the dishes. No making of beds. No scrubbing the bathroom. Of course, you may not do those things when you leave the dorm either, but that's beside the point. The world of work is so far from your mind that it might as well be nonexistent (besides, there's always graduate school). No job. No spouse. No kids. No mortgage. In a word: freedom. College life is almost too good to be true. It's a charmed existence.

Of course, it can't last. Your future extends beyond graduation and it doesn't look so promising. Suddenly you've got to convince an employer to give your liberal-arts-degreed self a job. Preferably a meaningful job with a good salary. Or at least a job with potential. O.K. then, any job. Clerk? $12,000 a year? Take it! You have to move back home with mom and dad. First payments on student loans are due in six months. Your college steady is in another state and it costs a fortune to fly out there. When you do go, you spend the first day getting reacquainted, the second day fighting, and the last day—well, it all depends on how the first two days went. Work's a drag—boredom, long hours, demanding people, measly paycheck. You feel like you're wasting your life but feel too trapped to do anything about it. In a flurry of excitement you decide to leave your job and travel for awhile. You "find yourself." Everything goes great until you get back, when your awakening doesn't seem to impress prospective employers. So, it's back to the job hunt, but what's even more confusing is you're not sure what you want to do with your life now. You're twentysomething, and you're floundering.

This project began when I was asked to give a short talk to a church group on "my own theology." The Sunday service had a short space for a member of the congregation to describe briefly their view of God, the universe, and the meaning of life. I had heard others describe nature, mathematics, and a more traditional Christian interpretation of Jesus Christ as their views of the ultimate.

The night before I was supposed to speak, I hadn't come up with anything that sounded very. . . well. . . religious. I was ready to throw in the towel and call the minister to tell him I wouldn't be ready. Because of some difficulties I'd experienced in recent years, I wanted little more than just to survive my twenties. But I pushed on, figuring that I could make something out of my story that people would be able to relate to. I found myself wincing more than once as I retraced my steps over the previous five years.

After college, in my desire to impose some direction on my life, I had plunged headlong into a demanding Ph.D. program in family therapy. Things had moved along very well for about two years before I started to stumble. As a young counselor in training I was making all the mistakes inexperienced trainees make, such as taking their clients' progress too personally and not drawing firm enough boundaries when clients acted inappropriately. These things created unanticipated aggravations, like calls at all hours from needy clients.

As uncertainty about my career choice grew, the one question that kept nagging at me was, what else would I do if I were to drop out of graduate school? I was beginning to sense that this kind of work wasn't for me, but wasn't dealing with my dilemma at all well. Instead of facing up to the task of recasting some of my plans and dreams and starting to explore again, I took the low road — basically, I began to party heavily. Great idea, eh?

Several months went by and, more out of desperation than anything else, I broke up with my girlfriend of three years. Somehow I thought a change would help. Another fabulous decision. The corrosive effects of the late nights, the break-up, and my career confusion combined to plunge me into despair. The partying started to catch up with me. I was no longer able to concentrate very well or experience pleasure.

Not long after, I was driving through Chicago on an overcast day after having dinner with my parents. They had plainly been upset about my impulsive decision to break up with my girlfriend. "Why did you do it? It's so unlike you to spring something like that on her so insensitively. What is going on with you?" they pleaded. Their words stung, and I didn't have a lot to say to them in return. Their disapproval made my uncertainty even worse. I stopped for gas on the way home and tried to make small talk with the cashier. He didn't seem to understand what I was saying. Sure, I'd been down before, but something was different this time. I felt as though the whole world was beginning to collapse in on me. As I drove through the flat Indiana farmland, spools of rain unwound on the stark brown fields. I felt like I was losing my mind.

A few weeks passed, and to the consternation of friends and family, I dropped out of graduate school and moved back home for awhile. I had always been an independent person, a good student, and even had a creative streak, but I kept sinking. I was cynical and morose; friends and family found me intolerable to be around. Even I couldn't stand to be around me, and I didn't have any choice. For five months it dragged on — the longest months of my life. Then I hit bottom. For about a month I thought of ending it all. I never actually got close, but it's natural under such circumstances to look for a way out. I was just holding on.

Eventually, after some persuasive nudging from my folks, I found a sublet and moved out. Not long after, I found a job, and the combination of being out of the house and working again helped me get back on my feet. I had a lot of work left to do before I would feel like my "old self" again, but I was on the road to recovery from my depression.

As I look back on it, I made two big mistakes. One was not recognizing that I had a career confusion problem and wasn't acting appropriately in response to it. Narrowing down the field of career options is more a process of elimination than the result of inspired callings from above. What I didn't do was bring a focus to my problem. I sensed that I didn't want to be a psychotherapist, but I didn't follow through on searching for something else that excited me.

The second major mistake was not handling my crisis in a healthy way. Clean living is important during periods of stress. All of my partying was basically just an avoidance tactic. If I had kept that up, there was little chance I would have emerged from my problems in good shape.

At any rate, by the time I was asked to speak at the church the worst part was over. As noted above, I had moved back out of my parent's house and landed a job. With these moves came new friends, a new sense of opportunity, and most importantly, emotional stability. I was still laboring under the effort to come to terms with my failure, my devastated self-esteem, and the loss of a promising career and a scholarship. But I was hanging in there and doing what I had to do to get back on track.

What did I say at the talk? I can't seem to recall much of it, but I wasn't afraid to let my vulnerability show. I told stories about how confusing career and relationship decisions can be, and how easy it is not to be honest with ourselves.

Introduction

I quoted a favorite folk-rock duo of mine, the Indigo Girls. I said that I didn't have any highfalutin principles or theologies, and that my sights were set no higher or lower than surviving this bizarre time of life.

The warmth of the responses I received to the talk inspired me to build on it. Several parents even approached me after the talk and asked me to send a copy to their confused offspring! I suspected that I might be onto something that could be helpful to others and continued to develop my ideas. This book is the result of the three years of work it took to pull this project together.

During my troubled time I had gone to the bookstore for help and had come up with nothing. The books I found focused too much on an individual's attitude and not enough on real-life issues. I felt particularly lost because the world around me didn't seem to recognize my problems. Was I the only one struggling through my twenties? I needed some more elementary help with making sense of my painful experiences and self-doubts. This book is offered up to help meet that need.

A disclaimer: we twentysomethings are a diverse group of individuals, and obviously the experience of each person in any group is unique. Generalizations, while capturing similarities, obscure differences. Everyone is shaped by innumerable influences: class, race, religion, ethnic background, personality, family, economic conditions, and so on. The categorizations I employ (not only of twentysomethings, but also of baby boomers and other broadly sketched groups) are merely used in the service of ordering my impressions.

It's my belief that these generalizations about our characteristics and attitudes distinguish us as a group that's sufficiently cohesive for general discussion. I would never want to pretend to be a representative of my generation. We have as many representatives as we do members. I only hope my comments will be taken as the reflections of one member who has been curious enough to make some observations, through the course of informally interviewing many people in their twenties over the course of several years. But all the opinions and judgments within are my own and should be taken as such and only as such.

I began by talking to anybody and everybody about what sort of experiences they had while living through their twenties, and tried to tease out both what this period in life is all about in a generic sense, and what coming of age in this particular era is like. The numbers of people I poked and prodded probably ran up into the four or five hundreds. What follows is some of what I've learned. It would not have been possible without the people who bravely shared intimate and often painful details of their lives with me. It was and is a rare privilege to share in their stories and in turn to try to do them justice here.

A charmed existence is by definition temporary. Mine ended at the same moment the idea for this book was born. In writing it I arrived at the following conclusion: there are basically two kinds of twentysomethings in the world, gliders and strugglers. This book is for strugglers seeking to polish their technique and for gliders who suspect that it's only temporary.

ONE

Huh?

MUDDLING through our twenties is like being out in the wilderness with a torn map and an unreliable compass. Just when we feel sure of our way, our paths take unexpected turns, skitter off the map, or dead-end completely. We lose our bearings. We don't know where to look for guidance. There are dozens of signposts and they all point in different directions: success, independence, social conscience, and respectability all clamor for our attention. Uncertainty can hobble us, or at the very least break our stride. Suddenly we bump up against the realities of surviving in the big bad woods all alone. Maybe we just left college, and we miss that secure, summer-camp feeling. Well, now camp is over. It's easy to become intimidated: good paths are hard to find, and the other hikers play for keeps. Everywhere people seem to be trying to weasel us out of our trail mix.

As recently liberated adolescents, we know this is the time to start making some of our dreams happen: go to exotic places, meet interesting people, find exciting work, have our own apartment or car, and find mentors who want to help us. But it's also true that the mighty dollar looms large. It costs big money to live on more than pasta, pay for health insurance, dress respectably, keep a car on the road, date, and outfit a place with furniture. For this reason and others, many of us move back home for awhile. We can't even afford to travel, let alone come up with the cash for graduate school.

Thinking too much about our biggest problem — figuring out what to do with our lives — can leave us feeling torn and confused. Many of us have come to dread being prodded with "The Question" at social gatherings and family reunions. "So what exactly *are* you doing these days?" We mumble and fidget and suddenly see fit to refresh our drinks. We sense that it's bad form to admit to shapeless career plans, or worse yet, unemployment. After all, this is America, where normal people "make something of themselves." If we don't play the chutes-and-ladders game of success, we are somehow suspect. But as we leave college, we're discovering there's no welcome mat being laid out to our economic future. Despite this, we're supposed to have it all together, or at least *act* like we do.

But even those who profess to having direction often have doubts. Underneath our brave fronts, we're all a little afraid — afraid that we won't measure up, afraid that we won't have friends, afraid that we have come of age in the land of opportunity only to find it in crisis. Isn't it about time we quit being so polite about what we're up against?

As young adults we begin to undergo the "normal" traumas of looking for work, coming up with a plan for our futures, and testing our interests, our dreams, and ourselves. We're searching for a sense of fit with the world. We may fantasize about picking coffee beans in Nicaragua, conquering Wall Street, and writing poetry in the woods all in the course of a single week. We are open to a myriad of conflicting social pressures: grow up, party down, get married, stay single, get ahead, speak out for what's right, mind your own business, save the earth, save your breath.

But this isn't the whole story, either. There is plenty to be optimistic about as we enter our twenties. We have real freedom and real time (if not real money); freedom to explore ourselves, relationships, ideas, and the world at large. That's enough to keep anyone busy for a couple of lifetimes.

When else can we dance all night, go out for breakfast at five in the morning, have intimate conversations on street corners, road trip on a whim, and pursue mountain climb-

10

ing with wild abandon? Here we are at exhilaration central. New music, new places, new apartments, new love — we rock and roll to them all. If someone crowds our space, all we have to do is say "hey, it's my movie, so back off."

In the pages that follow I will try to give a balanced account of what I've learned about our generation. Flip-flopping between basic survival tasks, making or postponing major life decisions, exploring, and just plain having fun has all have their tensions and attractions. (Attrensions?)

Speed Bump

Our first few steps as adults can be some of the most perplexing. Where to live? What to pursue? How to pursue it? With what support? What if we feel like impostors? Everything is so new. Many people never anticipated how hard that first speed bump of adult life would be. One friend related: "I had a job interview yesterday, and I think I really blew this one. It just didn't go well at all. There I was, blue suit, asking the interviewer if she minded if I take notes like I always do, you know, trying to win some early brownie points. So then I open my briefcase and Boop! My roommates had put my soccer cleats in there as a prank. The sourest smelling soccer cleats in the league were the first impression I made."

We may feel unprepared for and unnerved by the waiting, the uncertainty, and the frustration involved in the transition away from school. You can only take so much rejection before it starts to feel personal. One woman's boyfriend put it this way: "She's been diligently searching and interviewing for at least a year and a half now, has a solid degree, and nothing! It's unreal. I've never seen anything like it."

"You have your ideals, and you need to survive," a recent engineering graduate said. "Sometimes the pressure to start my career and yet move so that my girlfriend and I can stay together — it's all a bit much." What if a smooth transition away from school and into the world eludes us? What if the reception committee that we hoped would be waiting to embrace our goals and affirm the importance of our interests is nowhere in sight?

Is anyone interested in helping us better understand what we're up against? Who is old enough to have a perspective yet young enough (at heart anyway) to be able to relate? A special education teacher and parent of a 28-year-old expressed it this way: "I admire a lot of young people because they're really on their own. When I left college in the early Sixties, I was married and so were most of my peers. I remember a couple of women in my sorority house who hadn't married yet and just took off for California and became teachers and even got their own apartment! That was considered radical to us then! The point is, whatever happened to me — good, bad, or indifferent — there was always this person there. Now, I'm not saying that getting married young is what everyone should run out and do, but I will say that I always had support during those years. And frankly, I sometimes wonder how young single people manage."

How do we manage? It seems like we are warned about and expect the difficulties of adolescence and mid-life, but nobody really talks about the "tortuous twenties." What else do we need to learn about the "real" world beyond the responsibility of bills and occasional rough handling on the job? Finding support, juggling multiple roles, dealing with personally chaotic times: how does one steer through them? One woman wrote from Africa, where she was working in Niger with the Peace Corps: "I feel like the only recognizable track I'm on is the one I see behind me. I'm not doing what either of my parents did and I don't feel like I can see very far ahead. Where am I going? I've thought of settling (here), but ultimately I know I have to reconcile myself to a life in the States. It's just such an adjustment coming back from this kind of culture. Whenever I come home I just sit and stare

at the wall for a month. It's weird having what you leave behind as your only reference point."

Somehow we are supposed to just make our own way.
Sure we will manage to stumble through somehow, but how
can we more quickly sort out which paths are worth taking?
What are some concrete steps we can take to improve our situation?

Art with a Capital "F"

"Do you feel creative in your work?" I asked an acquaintance now working in advertising in Manhattan. "Ho-ho,
yeah," he replied, "it's art with a capital 'f'." It's ironic how
this time of turmoil and empty pockets is promoted by ad-
vertisers as the idyllic image of life as it should be: free, spon-
taneous, exhilarating, and vibrant. On bad days, these images of unfettered youthful bounciness seem designed to
appeal only to older viewers with slack memories. The con
fusion of not knowing what to do with our lives and the lack
of connection we may feel to the adult world make our
generation's transition tougher. Maybe the future isn't so
promising. Many of us somehow feel that the real world is
gearing up to punish us. Our anxiety is compounded if it
seems that some of our peers are racing on ahead.

As the realities of the world of work seep in, it's often a
case of too-much too-soonism: bills to be paid, major decisions to make, day-to-day reality to be faced, relationships
that soar and then nosedive. To many people in school, the
working world barely seems real. But the lessons come hard
and fast once we dive in and start floundering around.

Our twenties are about passing our flounderings off as
progress just long enough to learn to swim. As a fellow I
shared a breakfast-counter with quipped, "When you're in
your twenties you can screw up and still laugh it off. In your
thirties, that's harder to do." So, we've got that going for us.

Adult World

For a variety of reasons, then, many of us feel befuddled as we emerge from college to enter that heavy-duty theme park, Adult World. We're tall enough now to gain entrance to almost any ride. Given the choices, then, how do we know which ones to try? Should we take the fun rides? The scary? The corny but safe kiddie rides? Or should we start a mass movement to engineer new ones?

As time goes on, we begin to figure out that the "perfect ride" is a myth. Even people who report a high level of satisfaction with their careers have moments (or weeks or months) of real ambivalence and dissatisfaction. It's not like we leave college and someone says, "Here's your life!" and we get in and drive off. It's a constantly unfolding process that requires making tough choices, disciplining ourselves, and dealing with unforeseen snags.

But basically, it's good news. We live in a country where we are free to construct a life that we can learn to like, even if we don't love it at first. We can get started on the long pro-

---

☐ Ten Great Things About Being In Your Twenties

- ■ Putting $2 worth of gas in your car at a time
- ■ Parental assistance of a concrete nature
- ■ Road trips in reliable automobiles
- ■ Ramen noodles, especially that fifth night in a row
- ■ Waking up in a lot of beds we never made
- ■ Having the best set of pals, ever
- ■ Getting that first job
- ■ Getting into graduate school
- ■ Succeeding at either or both of the above
- ■ Great third dates

---

ject of defining our values and having fun. On good days, it is a grand adventure — there is a lot to look forward to.

The bad news is, we may never be this secure again. It's not uncommon for people to reach age twenty-four and look around at their lives and say, "this is what I yearned for all through adolescence?" Eventually we will grow more relaxed with ourselves, although our impatience for that golden day can be excruciating at times.

Focus

One of the keys to achieving that relaxation is focus: focus on our work, on who we are, on enjoying life, and on the values we want to bring to the world. If we don't develop the ability to focus within ten years or so, we run the risk of waking up when we're forty and saying, "Oh my God! I forgot to get a job!" One man had this particular realization during a month that he spent 200 feet up in a redwood tree. Sponsored by an activist group, he was "defending" the tree from logging, and had plenty of time up there to think. Since college he had maintained a paper route and pretty much lived off public support. In his hippie days, that was what a lot of people who rejected the "system" did, but he realized it was no longer acceptable to him. He resolved to pursue a career in computers and is now gainfully employed and satisfied with the transition. Which is not to say that redwood sitting is bad work; it was just time for him to make a change. Once we get beyond our concern over being too yuppie, many of us realize that developing a focus is something we need to do to get what we want out of life.

We're not stupid. We see the discrepancy between what is *believed* to be important, desirable, and possible in America and the way things really are. There is a silent rebellion against what the prevailing order asks and what it seems to offer. This is one reason why, in this day and age, being twentysomething is more difficult than adolescence. What's a little identity confusion compared to chronic underemployment? Yet as we flounder around feeling alternately overwhelmed and excited, we're searching for a civilized way to figure out what to do about it.

Believe it or not, we are well suited to the problematic Nineties. We are a reality-based generation, not sucked in by either extreme of materialism or idealism. Pragmatism is the middle course we're steering. We twentysomethings, who can't remember the assassination of JFK but do remember a time when MTV didn't exist, grew up with television and know something of the spin doctor's trade. We can decode the media and its attempts to market and manipulate. We are keeping many a market researcher up at night. Some commentators claim that if the big U.S. car companies can't figure out how to sell to us, they're basically sunk.

We went to college in the decadent Eighties and grew up in the "Me Decade" of the Seventies. I can't remember a time when Americans weren't into "Me." Four-fifths of divorced people from our parents' generation report that they were happier after they divorced, but most of us, their children, didn't feel that way at all. And even as we speak, the national debt is being balanced on our backs.

Some of the issues unique to twentysomethings in the Nineties include the ugly prospect of downward mobility, the harsh reality of encroaching social pathologies, and what appears to be a frightening increase in personal emotional turmoil. Some studies I will treat later suggest that if we are ever going to have an emotional disorder, we are most likely to have it in our twenties. Others suggest that depression and suicide are on the rise among young people. In California, a researcher for the insurance industry discovered that in the Eighties stress-related claims went up by over 110 percent, compared with only a 15 percent rise in non-stress-related claims. A large drug company did a survey and found that twentysomethings had more headaches

than their thirtysomething and fortysomething counterparts. When asked why, respondents cited reasons such as
not getting enough sleep, having too much to do, broken automobiles, wanting a better job, putting up with relatives,
being broke, and so on. Sound familiar?

Reinventing Ourselves in a Reinvented World

More discussion about what's really going on among people
in their twenties might help us to see the zigzags, course
changes, and broken lines our lives describe as more normal.
If people are going to be strange, odds are their weirdest tan-
gents will occur during their twenties. The combustible
combination of freedom, hormones, and lack of cash can
create bizarre and outrageous experiments: Young Republican becomes biker-babe; milkman becomes college basketball star; rock and roll guitarist moves his band to New York,
takes up photography, and finally becomes a substance-
abuse counselor. These stories aren't fiction. They are the
lily-pads that a few of the people interviewed for this book
landed on as they hopped through their twenties.

We reinvent ourselves, American-style, as we experiment
with new friends, lovers, hats, hang-outs, destinations, theologies, and lifestyles. We have the freedom to pursue different interests and to portray ourselves however we want, although the lack of rootedness that allows us to do so may
spell trouble for some of us. Nevertheless, that freedom *does*
exist, as does a high level of tolerance and acceptance of "alternative" life choices.

At any rate, as we enter this process of simultaneously ad-
justing to both changes in our own lives and the shifts occur-
ring in the world, our major task becomes clear: to reiterate,
we have to bring a focus to the blurry parts of our lives. We
must figure out how to get beyond our ambivalence and be

able to say, *this* is what I am committed to. *This* is my work. *This* is how and where I'm going to earn a living for the time being. *This* is when I stop wearing my Hard Rock Cafe T-shirt. *This* is what is, and who is, important to me in the long run. And *this* is what I have to do to follow through.

But developing this focus is tougher for some of us than it is for others. If a person doesn't know what they want to do career-wise, then they have to develop a means for learning and exploring themselves, their abilities, and what's available to them in life. In this sense, "adulthood" is really not the monolithic state we may have thought. "Exploring" and "searching" are fundamentally different from "executing a plan" and "following through." Those people who from the age of eight know they want to be in computers or chemistry can make the chronically confused green with envy. Life isn't fair. It doesn't fall in place as easily for some of us as it does for others. Sooner or later, we put aside our search for the "perfect" job and just plunge in. This is the time to develop our street smarts. We need hands-on experience now to complement our formal education: gut science, baby.

The Parent Trap

The feeling many of us associate with leaving our families for life on our own is a mixture of love, loyalty, irritation, and pain. It's easy to get caught up in old family patterns and problems. The perspective we develop as we get farther from home brings fresh insight and sophistication. We learn about other families and this helps us to appreciate what is positive about our own. But we also may begin to mourn the ways in which we were deprived or hurt by our parents. We may begin to feel some healthy anger. We have a lot to work through when it comes to our parents; we'll probably hear their voices cajoling, consoling, advising, and nagging us for the rest of our lives — inside our heads. The truth is, we may still be afraid of disappointing them.

Facing the fact that there is no real human security in life is frightening. Once we say goodbye to our parents, there will be no one there to say that everything will be O.K., that everyone lives happily ever after, and would you like to hear another bedtime story? We need to build some framework into our lives that allows us to take the world's disorder and senseless suffering into account. If we don't, we won't know how to reach out when they touch our own lives.

Our Advantages

We are in the singular position of being able to benefit from some of America's most radical experiments and disasters, and also from the sturdiness of its more venerable traditions. Although we tend to be ambivalent about how to proceed, at least we're not unthinkingly plunging into whatever stupid fad happens to come along next. We can draw concrete conclusions, good and bad, from witnessing the fallout that's resulted from the Sixties and the Eighties, those two big decade-long American feeding frenzies. A smattering: the sexual revolution is over and everybody lost. Excessive consumerism is nothing to base a life on, and shaky economics to boot. Leveraged buy-outs, as well as the other manifestations of fast and loose financial exploitation that distinguished the Eighties, exact too great a human cost. Children need limits and guidelines, not neglect in the name of unconstricted freedom. Basic ecological conscientiousness — like recycling and riding our bikes to work — makes sense.

And more personal lessons come to mind: a noted psychology professor confessed that she felt compelled to marry her first husband because he was the first person she ever slept with. Few of us would make the same mistake today. A young man saw the toll his father's career as a litigator has taken on him and opts for less stressful, or at least less adversarial work. A young woman cringed at her mother's frantic juggling of roles as an accountant and homemaker. She began to resent it when she came home on holidays to find mom racing around while her father turned into "Sofa Man" after work. Needless to say, she makes sure that her boyfriend pulls his weight around the house.

We can learn from what we admire about the preceding decades and try to incorporate those lessons into our lives. There are a multitude of choices available to us now, and this trend is reflected in our fashions and politics. If we want to be very corporate, or very radical, or very artsy, we can, without feeling that we're bucking (or have to buck) any dominant cultural trends. These "subcultures" exist side by side along with a lot of others in a fairly coherent fashion, and we can straddle several at a time if we wish.

Challenges

Yet questions remain. Can we find a civilized way to deal with the changes our society is undergoing as the American economic pie shrinks? Are there alternatives through which we can reaffirm what is positive about our society and help to reverse its encroaching degeneration? Perhaps there is ground for more creativity and choice now, but this is all taking place against the backdrop of an increasingly scary world.

More and more of us who planned to be on the yuppie track will find ourselves off it in the years to come. Perfectly competent and talented young people will not be able to launch their brilliant careers, or at least not in the ways they imagined. But plenty of people have fashioned very creative careers in the absence of a job in their original field.

We will need to find ways of getting interested in other things: to make our own way, perhaps a little against the grain. So you're not off to a whiz-bang start in the career department — big deal. Take a trip, try out for a play, decide you want to correspond with twenty people regularly and do it. Cultivate more friendships, volunteer, start a book discussion group, or even your own business. The fact is that we can lead enriching and fulfilling lives even if our initial aspirations don't seem to be working out quite as we thought. Besides, with the Nineties job market shaping up as it is, we may be in for some long-term floundering if we don't adjust. No one is taking us aside at graduation parties and saying, "I want to say just one word to you: watercolors." (The plastics business ain't doin' so hot.)

Our generational predecessors have committed themselves to being good at creating a national defense system, developing advanced medical technology, and building and refining a nation-wide network of fine research universities, among other things. What will our generation contribute? Will we, for instance, prove that we can deal progressively with our nation's growing set of social problems (the burgeoning underclass, skyrocketing health care costs, the decline in public education)? Will we be able to create likable lives without the material underpinnings represented by the "American Dream?" Can we develop the courage to ask the hard questions: who's hurting, what's hurting them, and what, in all kindness and decency, can we do about it? Can we learn from other countries that have dealt successfully with similar social problems? There doesn't seem to be any dominant mode of life emerging yet in the Nineties, and this means that the opportunity to build alternatives to past modes still exists.

There is plenty to keep us preoccupied on the immediate, personal level of our lives as well. It would be tragic to pass up intriguing opportunities and avoid risks for fear of screwing up. Just like it's a baby's job to cry, it's our job to push our limits, take risks, and not be afraid to fail. We must fail and fail at a lot of different things if we want to learn. Failure happens, so we might as well get used to it and not be afraid of it. Unfortunately, the stigma that surrounds failure in our pain-avoidant culture can make us feel needlessly paranoid. Pushing beyond that stigma and learning from our own experiences of pain and failure (as well as joy and fulfillment) is a major step in coming to terms with the vagaries of adult life.

"If someone told me when I was twenty what I'd be doing when I was thirty, I never would have believed them," was the most oft-repeated refrain I heard in my interviews. Things have this uncanny way of working themselves out if we give them the time and attention they need. Many people reported that their lives finally settled down as they reached thirty or so. As we wrestle with hard choices, take on more responsibility, and learn to live with ambiguity, we have a lot to look forward to.

Openness

One of the best things about being in our twenties is our openness to experience. We have not been around long enough to become too jaded, yet we are beyond our blushing years. Many thinkers and writers have commented on this openness, and many artists created their most famous works in their twenties. Michelangelo's "David" and Einstein's theory of relativity were both fashioned when their creators were twenty-six. The poets Byron, Shelley, and Dylan Thomas wrote their most beautiful and original verses in their twenties. Mathematicians and philosophers often burn brightest in their youth. This anecdotal evidence supports the notion that we have certain abilities at this stage of life that are not the product of experience or knowledge. One wonders how many of the brilliant jazz musicians who committed suicide (or drugged themselves into oblivion) in their early thirties despaired that their creative peak might be over.

When we enjoy that easy fluency with others that is the

mark of good friendship and our openness has room to roam, exciting things begin to happen: exhilarating bull sessions, all-stops-pulled pick-up basketball, silly parties, group projects and retreats, charitable works — the list is endless. Our energies and enthusiasms have yet to be neutered by cynicism or too much hard experience. Despite our coming of age in the Eighties, numbness and predictability didn't seem to gain too strong a foothold in our hearts and minds.

Poet John Berryman's first wife, Eileen Simpson, described the special bonds of friendship that can arise in our twenties in her book, *Poets in their Youth*, when writing of Berryman's friendship with Dylan Thomas: "While John and Dylan had met infrequently after their week together in London, they had been intimate during that period in a way for which only the young have the time, energy and freedom." This allowed them to be close whenever they were together. Unfortunately, this openness also makes us acutely vulnerable to life's let-downs and disillusionment, as the rest of Berryman's young adult life illustrated. He spent most of it unsure of his talent, broke, and anxious. But despite his — and our — travails, there are few times that match our twenties for sheer vibrancy.

Dignity

Strengthening your sense of personal dignity will help you get through your twenties and beyond with power and style. Self-help books identify numerous steps towards healthy personhood: "knowing who you really are," "self-love," "self-actualization," and "being whole." Most of these faddish phrases have already atrophied into cliches. Dignity, however, is a word that still connotes self-respect, confidence, and humanity, suffused with a sense of grace.

Placing a high value on dignity allows us to cultivate healthy desires that do not impinge on others. Manipulation and degradation of other people simply won't do. If you have dignity, it follows that you also do what you can to enhance the dignity of others. And this goes for everyone: boss and employee, teacher and student, parent and child. Roy Stryker, a bureaucrat in the Farm Security Administration, compiled over 270,000 pictures of farmers and sharecroppers during the Great Depression. In their faces he saw dignity at war with despair. "Maybe I'm a fool," he said. "But I believe that dignity wins out. When it doesn't, then we as a people will become extinct."

It is our challenge to be brave enough to stretch beyond ourselves; to do things that flesh out our souls; to transcend a life of one damn neurotic or banal episode after another; to revel in both life's seriousness and its essential absurdity. Make everything you do align with your own sense of dignity. This means treating yourself and others with respect.

Learning how to heighten your awareness of dignity is not a random process. There are better and worse ways to make the connections you need to make. People do heighten their sensibilities, become more profoundly in tune with their worlds, enjoy the rewards of hard work and accomplishment, and increase their capacity for love.

Will We Ever Be This Silly Again?

It's doubtful. I would never want to sell short the excitement of this vivid time of life. When will we ever have more time for hanging out with our friends? When will we be as adventurous, or as vulnerable? Ultimately we may not remember our twenties as the best time of our lives, but we need to give them the chance to be.

The Nineties Environment

Some people can spend an inordinate amount of time covering the distance between school and the adult hereafter. Our twenties are neither "maturity practice" nor a sort of weigh station on the road to a settled, stable life. They are filled with long detours that are not really detours because they don't necessarily get us back to where we thought we were going. And this has never been more true than in the Nineties. As the British group Jesus Jones sings, "I saw the decade end/When it seems the world could change/In the blink of an eye. . . but if feels good just to be alive. . . Right here, right now/There is no other place I want to be/Watching the world wake up from history."

Perhaps there has never been a time when mental age (or how old you feel) has been so out of sync with chronological age. It used to be that simple observance of social rites and gestures made you an adult. No longer. The good news is, many of us are now able to grow up according to our own psychological clock. The bad news is, it's hard to know where we stand in relation to the world.

Onward and Downward

We can no longer ignore the fact that as a generation we face the prospect of downward mobility. Demographers have christened us N.I.K.E.s (No-Income Kids with Education).

Not a few of us will have more degrees than both of our parents combined yet will never reach their level of income. Salaries and bonuses are shrinking in almost all fields, and oftentimes don't even keep up with inflation. Our generation is the poorest age bracket in American society, with one in five of us living in poverty. Half of the total population of uninsured Americans are under the age of twenty-five. In 1967 the young male wage earner made 74 percent of what his older male coworker made. In 1988, that figure was 54 percent. An economist recently reported on National Public Radio that 20 percent of the U.S. population keeps doing better and better, and the other 80 percent worse and worse. Do we throw our life out of balance to try to get into that 20 percent, or take a look around at our society and try to help out? Can we do both?

Some recent research suggests that single-breadwinner families in the Fifties made more when cost-of-living adjustments are figured in than double-breadwinner families make today. That startling statistic underlines the fact that most families don't have a choice about whether both spouses work or not. Sure, we forget that our parents struggled, lived in closet-sized apartments, and survived on tuna sandwiches when they started out too. But there is more to it than that now.

A college student is considering a career as an administrator in handicapped services. His research reveals that he can eventually hope to make $30,000 a year once he attains a degree and some experience. He begins to consider law school. The National Association of Homebuilders estimates that it takes an income of at least $37,000 to be able to afford a modest, median-priced home. And forget about New York or Southern California, where you can hardly rent in a safe neighborhood on that kind of income. It takes nearly a six-figure income to achieve what used to be considered "middle-class" living. As writer Barbara Ehrenreich puts it: "All I can say is that there is something grievously wrong with a culture that values Wall Street sharks above social workers, armament manufacturers above artists, or for that matter, corporate lawyers above homemakers."

There is a lot of baggage bound up in downward mobility in terms of how we think about ourselves as Americans. The notion of upward-mobility — that hard-work will be rewarded by steady increases in income and status — is linked to our characteristically American faith in the possibility of continuous growth and progress. We're not used to thinking in terms of limits and cutbacks. We as a nation place enormous stress on these notions of unlimited potential.

And this is to say nothing of the personal shame downward mobility entails for many of us. We may have heard cautionary tales about relatives who "blew it" with drink or bad investments or something. We may have heard them described as living in "reduced" circumstances, often isolated from family and friends. The larger moral, whatever compassion we may feel for that person initially, isn't lost on us. Get ahead, kid! Or at least hang on to your current position and do your family proud.

This isn't necessarily a bad message. After all, parents have a legitimate right to expect you to be financially self-sufficient. But upward mobility will be available to fewer and fewer of us, and that hurts. Having come of age in the Eighties, we're not used to thinking small. As one recent well-to-do college graduate said, "I don't have any great career plans at this point, but I wouldn't be caught dead living in one of those trailer parks. I'll rent for the rest of my life if I have to." Social pressures to "succeed" in the mobility sense are intense, and the feelings we'll have about making less than our parents will be difficult for many of us.

There are more than a few indications that we are coming to the end of a confident and robust time when prosperity was taken for granted by many Americans. These ideals will be put to a severe test during our lifetimes, for international economic realities will no longer support this notion of unlimited growth. The standards on which we base our sense of progress in life will have to undergo some major changes if we want to avoid bitterness and the feeling of not measuring up. The economic fluctuations our generation will be subject to are due to structural, and not necessarily personal, failures and limitations. But many of us will find it hard not to confuse the two.

Issue One: Instant Gratification

Three major issues have distinguished the social context of our generation's coming of age. The first is our culture's emphasis on instant gratification. It's the "you-want-it, you-got-it" syndrome, without having to do any work. Mark Knopfler of Dire Straits captures this attitude in his song about warehouse workers thinking how easy playing guitar in a big rock group would be, where there's "money for nothing/and chicks for free." The over 6,000 promotional images and messages we are exposed to every day testify to how deeply conditioned we are in this respect. As Carrie Fisher wrote in *Postcards From The Edge*, "Instant gratification isn't soon enough." However, the combination of downward mobility and our love of instant gratification can be hell on one's bank account.

It may be old-fashioned to talk about things like delayed gratification, but if we want to work full-time and hang onto a credit card, it's pretty important. *Real* gratification can only come if we learn to delay short-term gratification. Some people talk a lot about becoming sharp lawyers or owning their own businesses or scaling up the Madison Avenue executive chain. Not all of them are willing to put in the work. This willingness becomes crucial when, as they say in the automotive industry, the rubber hits the road.

Issue Two: Choice

The second major development that has made growing up and making good decisions more difficult is the multiplicity of choices we face. With modern communications, the loosening of strict gender prohibitions, greater personal mobility, and the mind-boggling diversity of new information and service industries has grown a huge increase in occupational and life choices. College sophomores now sit around munching pizza, and instead of just saying to themselves, "Let's see, there's Law, Medicine, or Business," they are continuing ". . . and Computer Hacking, New Age Bodywork, Health Care, Peace Corps, Marine Corps, 1–800-Teach-America, Nonprofits, Software Publishing, Stand-up Comedy, Teaching English Abroad. . . ." Some surveys indicate that 60 percent of us wish we had fewer choices. We might legitimately question the quality of the choices available, considering how many of us will have to fall back on scut jobs while we hope the economy will give us a shot at greener pastures.

Maturity lies in good choices made and commitments kept. As long as we're still actively considering doing sixteen different things, it's hard to feel like we're becoming more grounded. The problem with having lots of choices is that the stakes seem higher. Before, choosing x was hard because that meant you couldn't do y. Now, if you do x, then you can't do y, z, or w! Most of us would rather have too many choices than too few, but here's the catch: decision-making is difficult and feeling overwhelmed with choices increases this difficulty. The truth is there will always be trade-offs. Flip-flopping between too many options may make us postpone an important decision to the point where a bad decision is made for us by default.

Growing up has become more complicated than many of us ever thought possible. We don't have the guidance or the confidence (or even the indulgence) that previous generations may have had. Before standardized tests and cut-offs were instituted, lots of people in previous generations were winked at and passed on from grade to grade to college to first job even if they couldn't do math or write a business letter. Not so with us. We are the most poked, prodded, tested, and retested generation ever, and if we thought it was bad for us, think of the poor little buggers just trying to get past the fifth grade now. And that means that more of us know the good and the bad news about where and how we measure up.

Issue Three: Family

The third major cultural issue buffeting us is the vast transformation in the structure of the family. We have grown up in or among families rocked by dissolution. Young adults today simply don't have as much stability in their backgrounds as they used to. The divorce rate, as we all know, is frighteningly high. The strains involved — custody arrangements, remarriages, new step- and half-sibling relationships, new homes, and divided loyalties — are now more the rule than the exception. We live in the Brave New World of the Blended Family. Divorce will send shock waves through any family, affecting the personal, social, and financial lives of the parents, the children, and the grandparents as well.

Data from the Census Bureau confirms this continuing trend. In 1970, over 70 percent of American households were made up of married couples compared to 56 percent in 1990. The number of non-family households rose more than 10 percent in the same period. There have even been an estimated 500,000 family "throwaways" born since 1961, kids whom no one would take responsibility for.

The upshot of all this is that more of us are coming from situations that don't provide as much structure and support as we'd like or need. We have to improvise something in the void that has come from the disappearance of lifetime family support. We lean on friends, or maybe move in with relatives, or form a new "survivors" clique with our siblings. But a person who has lost regular comfort and security will hesitate before they accept bits of comfort in the future. Even though we may feel a need for that comfort deeply, the pain involved in the prospect of having it removed again may feel like too great a risk.

Friendships, as great as they are, can't quite replace the strength and constancy of family bonds. There is something about being in a family that means you are in it through thick and thin, alienation and craziness, bankruptcy and bitter conflict. When we are really close to somebody, we say "Why, she's almost like family to me." As one man interviewed for this book opined, "Let's face it, friends will occasionally shit on you. They sleep with your girlfriend, dump you for other friends or a spouse and new family, or just generally become difficult and unpleasant. I'm one of those rare people who actually likes my parents, so I feel like I have a sense of security that allows me to take a fading friendship in stride. When I mention that I get along with my folks, people just kind of stare at me funny, like, huh? How does that work? Is that possible?"

One result of this transformation in family life is that a lot of people are mystified by intimacy. "I was totally clueless," a struggling young playwright confessed. "I thought marriage was about having a ring on my finger. Of course, me and my brothers and sisters *knew* we would never get divorced, but it's not until recently that I had any idea what actually making a marriage work was all about." Because of divorce and the dysfunctional character of many families that stay together, many of us don't know how to reach out and develop the kind of interdependence we need to thrive. There is hesitation born of betrayal, divided loyalty, inconstancy, and doubt. Many children of divorce either idolize or denigrate the institution of marriage. It's either supremely blissful or horribly nasty. This doesn't leave a lot of room in the middle for a realistic assessment of what marriage is all about.

A large body of psychological research supports the notion that people who have grown up in single-parent homes or who have had a parent abandon them have a harder time developing relationships later in life. This is not to say that a two-parent household is necessary or even ideal for young people to grow up and fashion lives of their own. There are plenty of screwed-up nuclear families. But let's be honest; stable situations with more than one adult present are easier on kids and adolescents.

Good information about life is hard to come by without the perspectives of people from various age groups. The "wisdom of the ages" — as anyone with open-minded grandparents will tell you — has value beyond the cliche. As family stability wanes, we may be more cut off from such wise and potentially very helpful people.

Who Me? Married?

According to the census, in 1988 77 percent of males and 61 percent of females between the ages of twenty and twenty-four had never married, compared to 55 percent of males and 36 percent of females in 1970. Similarly, for those between the ages of twenty-five and twenty-nine in 1988, 43 percent of men and 29 percent of women had never married, compared to 19 percent of men and 29 percent of women in 1970. These figures show how skittish we have become. It is a common and comic sight to see twentysomethings leaping to avoid garter belts and bouquets during those old rituals at weddings. Some of us make a career out of putting off commitment. One interviewee took twelve years to get through college and had postponed or backed out of engagements and weddings four times before he turned thirty.

During our interview one woman in her twenties reported, "I would never have kids in a first marriage." My only question is, what does she tell her first husband? The fact that someone could even come up with such a thought indicates that some of us have become cynical about the durability of intimacy. The marriage-for-life ideal is being replaced by the serial monogamy that we see all around us. The situation is getting so dire that even hopeless romantics catch themselves contemplating the benefits of arranged marriages.

Ambivalence

In my view, the word which best describes our generation is *ambivalent*. We tend to be suspicious of traditional institutions and hierarchies, and suspicious of organized politics, religion, and those motivated by the alleged purity of their "causes." We have had no Vietnam conflict, few if any major social upheavals, and no runaway idealism. Alex Keaton, the character played by Michael J. Fox on the sitcom "Family Ties," was representative of an era when many kids were more conservative than their parents. The youth vote supported Reagan, and the usual 10 percent majority that the Democrats used to enjoy among young people was reversed to favor the Republicans by as much as 18 percent in 1985.

The fact that during the Gulf War many people flip-flopped might be an indication of what's in store in the coming years: some liberals found themselves supporting the effort, and many conservatives opposed it. Our politics are less polemical, and the openly political brand of social activism seems to be on the wane. There is more of what I call human activism going on: people working on problems concerning amnesty, ecology, sexual harassment, animal rights, and other such causes.

We often define ourselves according to past reference points: the volatile Sixties, the fast-lane Eighties, and the "let's experiment" Seventies. Our fashions lack originality. They tend to be "retro-style" borrowings from other eras — cowboy boots matched with preppie sweaters. All-black apparel is as familiar as neon-hued athletic wear. This is one example of how instead of inventing broad new original trends we tend to be drawing from the past, in terms of both our values and our lifestyles. On many campuses, hippies in tie-dyes stand next to Young Republican preppies with tennis rackets. People whose religious views and conservative dress seems to have come right out of 1958 are becoming more visible. These are stereotypes, of course, but illustrate an emergent pluralism.

Perhaps our single most common characteristic is our nearly universal exposure to divorce. If our own parents didn't split, then we have been touched by the pain of friends, relatives, or neighbor families as they struggled through a divorce. Another segment of our generation came of age just when their parents became aware of their substance-abuse problems. Many of them were involved in the drug culture to varying degrees, or perhaps were heavy drinkers. The huge increase in public awareness about the dangers of addiction has affected many of us. Alcoholics Anonymous and other twelve-step organizations have become prominent on a national scale. These groups can provide a very important technology for young people trying to figure out how to become their own person despite home situations that often lack structure and support. They can teach us about issues like dependency, responsibility, guilt, and transcendence. These groups have helped literally hundreds of thousands, if not millions, of people fight their own destructive patterns of behavior. The twelve-steps aren't gospel, but their impact is hard to miss.

Expanded Notions

I believe we need to expand our conception of "health" to include notions of emotional and creative soundness, in terms of the choices we make about how to spend our time and energy. Reexamining what sanity and sound choices are may require us to put aside what society puts forth as ideal. Let's remember that physicians have one of the highest suicide rates among all occupational groups, and they supposedly have "made it." Committing suicide isn't "making it" in any sense of the word. The same could be said for our culture's emphasis on thinness and its sickening effects on women.

How we go about making life-choices is a fascinating if somewhat mysterious subject. We behave so stupidly sometimes, especially with the most important people in our lives. But it's also true that our culture gives us a lot of truly stupid messages about how to live life.

☐ **Ten Stupid Messages**

- You can never be too rich or too thin
- Wealth is a sign of intelligence and hard work
- If you find the "right" person, marriage will last forever
- Divorce is a quick-fix
- Buy Brand *X* and you will be a better person for it
- People of color are unknowable, alien, and dangerous
- Whoever dies with the most toys wins
- It is rewarding to worship celebrities
- Women are sex objects
- Men are success objects

Us and the Baby Boom

Our twenties can perhaps only be understood in a psycho-historical sense: the interaction of individual personalities, in all of their complexity, depth, and changeability, with new social, cultural, and economic conditions. We are inseparable from society and history. It makes us what we are, and we can only think and act within available frames of reference. What does it mean then, to be a young, educated, American, and to live and work in the last decade of the twentieth century? Living through the last two decades would be enough to make a lot of folks crazed. The values of the Sixties and Seventies were in many ways turned on their head in the Eighties. What strange cultural cross-currents took us from "see your own cervix" seminars to power networking luncheons? The media focused on the baby-boomers (those born between 1946 and 1960) while we were growing up. Their politics and consumer tastes have been endlessly popularized and dissected. The media has hugely distorted this group. First of all, not even a significant minority of the baby-boomers are upwardly mobile. Even fewer are brand-name fetishists. Nevertheless, the media expounds ad infinitum on their supposed work habits, sexuality, and child-rearing methods.

Am I the only one who's sick of all this? The media has hyped this generation to such a great degree that it's tricky to separate the myth from the reality. Their numbers, 72 million, make them so large and powerful a group that their practices and preferences have virtually defined each decade since the Sixties.

In comparison, the generation now between eighteen and twenty-nine numbers only 48 million. We live in the wake of the baby boom; as they proceed through life, what will distinguish the flotsam and jetsam of us twentysomethings?

36

Like quiet younger brothers and sisters, we lie in wait, looking for ways to be different from our older siblings.

So, who are we anyway? If the legions of self-appointed
experts on our generation that are swelling up from the ranks
of baby-boom journalists, social commentators, and psy-
chiatrists would let up with their unrelenting youth-bashing
just long enough to listen a minute, they might actually get
a clue. We've been told that we have low test scores, low
minds, inferior educations, and lousy attitudes for so long
that it would be a miracle if we could find it within ourselves
to take exception. Typically, we don't, but we will be quick
to shrug and add that "it was you that made us this way."
We have been labeled at different times "the know-nothing
generation," "shocking on the outside, unknowable on the
inside," "matter-of-fact about sex," "ruined," "lost," "dumb
and numb," "junky" and as having "herky-jerky brains."
One commentator charges us with starting "The New Cold-
ness," another with the "rising tide of mediocrity."

So who's got the attitude problem? It's a generational
conceit to look at the generation just behind one and call it
trashy. It makes those old hippies feel good when they say,
"young people today have no idealism." We know that—
considering the circumstances—we've got an awful lot going
for us, but many of our elders lack such confidence. They see
the country going to hell in our handbasket. Maybe there is
no convincing them of our uniqueness and strengths. But before they indulge in too much self-satisfied disappointment
over how we're turning out, they might take a moment to
fathom how disappointed *we* are in them and the punishing
world problems they've helped create.

Where We're Coming From

The interplay between the times we live in and our own psychology at this point in our life cycle forges our twenties ex-

perience. Just a few impressions: the generational psychology that I see evolving is marked by ambivalence toward both the past and the future. It has necessarily reduced economic expectations. It thinks too much. It is hounded by occasional paralysis. Steeped in the conviction that those who have come before have failed us, we are recognizing that the old conventional wisdom is waning, at the same time no new one seems to have emerged. Hippies, Druggies, and Yuppies have taken turns streaking across our social milieu but we have yet to put on our sneakers.

We are not so much questioning authority as ignoring or bypassing it. There is such a glut of hype and rhetoric being spouted out there, it's getting harder to cut through it all and get to some practical truths. In a recent article in a major business magazine, several seasoned executives were shocked at how often younger employees often just ignored the hierarchy at work and went to their boss's boss when there was

---

☐ Ten Great Bumper Stickers

(Thank god we haven't lost our sense of humor— always a sign that we'll pull through this confusing time one way or another.)

- I feel much better now that I've given up hope
- Celibacy: Just Do It
- Failure is Impossible
- How's my driving, 1–800–EAT–SH __ __
- Penny for your thoughts, twenty bucks to act them out
- Minds are like parachutes, they don't work unless open
- Every day is Auschwitz for the animals
- I'm not easy, but we can discuss it
- Life's too short for lousy communication
- I'm twentysomething, so please don't ask what I'm doing

---

some ethical problem or misunderstanding. More and more people are becoming suspicious of the "experts," who are overwhelmingly white male and who have so eagerly engineered consensus on political, social, and economic issues for the last half century. We are wondering how we can expand true democratic dialogue. Where will new and effective political and social frameworks emerge from? Independents? The Green Party? The New World Order? Morton Downey Jr.? The New Age? Dan Quayle? *Will* they emerge?

We need to forgive the world for not being perfect. Its problems are real, and the obstacles to resolving them and our sense of powerlessness seem equally real. We need to sort through what we really have control over and focus on that. But, we need to get on with it. How do we begin? To get a better understanding of what we're about, let's start by looking at some of the social and historical circumstances we grew up in.

The Way It Was

The roots of our ambivalence become more visible in light of several cultural cross-currents. We were coddled in homes that boasted one of the highest standards of living in American (if not all of) history. As one friend said upon graduating from high school, "sure we're spoiled, but we're not brats." And yet when we leave home, we find ourselves having to stretch just to pay basic bills. The loss of status inherent in being off the yuppie track is difficult for some of us. Economic pressures have been a part of our coming-of-age years, and we're not taking economic opportunity so much for granted anymore. Housing price inflation and stagnant wages have taken their toll.

We were yanked around by the tug of several cultural undertows. Our parents were brought up to embark on careers and start families as soon as possible. By the end of the Sixties, however, when today's twentysomethings were in their swaddling clothes, important changes in government, the economy, and social mores were afoot. These shifts began to reshape virtually all aspects of public and private life, altering our parents' values, expectations, and child-rearing methods.

The civil rights movement was in full swing, feminism was becoming a major public issue, opposition to the Vietnam War was strengthening, and a general distrust of government was growing even in traditionally conservative sectors of the nation. For some of us, televised images of the map of Vietnam were our very first political memory. For others, their first experience of a strong connection with political life was stirred by the vision of women like Betty Friedan and Gloria Steinem.

Though most of our parents had traditional upbringings, many of them were influenced by social experimentation and the personal growth movements of the late Sixties and Seventies. Some of our parents entered therapy for the first time — in groups, as couples, or individually. The personal growth movement plugged "doing your own thing." Sex was increasingly viewed as a recreational activity rather than a forbidden, sacred, or procreational one. Experiments like "open marriage" often proved to be miserable failures (if there ever was a contradiction in terms, that was surely it). We were guinea pigs in the laboratory of their new ideals, lifestyles, and attitudes toward parenting. Many of us were raised by the double-edged credo of the new liberated parents: "We want you to do whatever you want to do, as long as it's excellent." Others grew up in homes without rules, limits, or discipline because of the prevailing notion that children should not be controlled. We witnessed the fallout from these experiments first-hand; sometimes we *were* the fallout.

Even this fallout, however, is ambiguous. A rising divorce rate has taught legions of divorced people, their attorneys, therapists, children, and their children's therapists that divorce is shattering. On the flip side, there is research that supports the notion that couples who stay together even though they are miserable do even more damage to their kids. Divorce is easier to obtain; yet research repeatedly documents the "feminization" of poverty — most of the "new poor" are single mothers with custody of their children who after divorce suffer a drastic decline in their standard of living, many dipping below the poverty line.

We are victims of the spending sprees of the federal government in the Eighties. They have passed the debt onto us and our children. We have inherited a public health-care system cracking at the seams, a public attitude that expects schools and teachers to be miracle workers and a natural environment that simply won't take much more abuse. Public confidence in government is slack and voter participation is down. On the positive side, there are increased opportunities for women to enter the work force (although there is still a lack of government support for child care). And there is a greater tolerance of differing sexual orientations and gender roles.

We have grown up in fragmented, rapidly shifting times. The transitions in values and mores from the Sixties to the Nineties are baffling to many. And throughout these shifts, we have been given many mixed messages.

While we witnessed intense efforts in the Seventies to get away from traditional ways of doing things, we have also witnessed backlash attempts to recoup the "straw man" of tradition in the Reagan Eighties.

We are currently undergoing the tail end of this generational identity crisis. In the Sixties and Seventies, if you were not part of the solution, you were part of the problem. In the Eighties, not making "enough" money was perhaps the only sin. Now, we face the repair work needed after a decade of excessive individualism and materialism where the rich got richer and everybody else a little poorer.

Developing secure values eludes us. All we have known is shifting sands: there was a mountain of certainty here yesterday, wasn't there? With economic conditions and family relationships in so much upheaval, we keep asking, "What works?" Unfortunately, we are learning that attempted solutions to problems go on to create their own problems.

I don't mean to paint our generation as martyrs who have been permanently damaged by growing up in this particular

---

☐ Mixed Messages

- Committed relationships are binding and sacred
  Committed relationships are disposable

- Securing wealth is a sign of competence and good character
  Making a lot of money means you have superficial values

- Sex is for fun
  Sex is deadly

- Big government is the best way to run our big country
  Big government is wasteful and intrusive

- Staying home and being a wife and mother is good
  Women who stay at home aren't realizing their potential

- Working for social change is noble
  Social activists are idealistic and immature dreamers

- Drugs used recreationally are harmless fun
  Using drugs will ruin you and means that you are morally flawed

- Getting a job within the "system" means selling out
  Getting on the fast-track means you're one of the best and brightest

---

era. I would never want to give the impression that our coming of age has just been a series of one painful experience after another. We have had no more difficult a time than previous generations. And I would not want to convey the image that most people in their twenties are living through a personal hell. We have had no military drafts (yet) or severe economic depressions. We can indulge ourselves a lot during this decade without having to worry about people depending on us.

Yet, our growing-up years were indisputably different from those of previous generations. We are paying the price for all this change and discontinuity. Living in a world one perceives as untrustworthy, in a family seen as insecure and impermanent, all contributes to the hardening of an individual. Many of us are guilty of a callous and single-minded focus on our own survival to the neglect of the concerns of others.

Patchwork History

The geopolitical forces that are shaping the latter part of the twentieth century have been unleashed at a quicksilver pace and are integrating previously remote nations into a streamlined global network.

Russia is no longer an evil empire requiring containment by an aggressive and ever-vigilant National Security State. The Cold War is winding down and the Berlin Wall is history. We congratulate ourselves on the failure of the Communist system as though it were an affirmation of our way of life. We forget the price we have paid: the near-bankruptcy of our economy to pay for the weapons that were supposedly "deterring" the Russian Bear.

We are now floundering in the first major post-Cold War crisis: namely, how to reconstitute a United States government that can no longer be focused on outstripping a huge superpower adversary. Events in the Persian Gulf have further postponed this transition. Without the overarching goal of fighting communism, what should the government be doing with itself? Window-dressing at home and abroad seems to be the order of the day. On the economic front, thousands of jobs have been and are continuing to be exported to Asia and Latin America. What is left of our crumbling economic base? Wall Street? Wal-Mart? Our GNP is stagnating, and all over the world people perceive America's influence as waning.

Where will we find the certainty we need to act? How do we balance our commitment to coping with the complex social problems around us against our desire for financial security? These are complex problems not amenable to sloganizing. We have fewer morally clear positions to take. The environment will not heal itself, however much we rant and rave. Its exploitation is deeply connected to our expected standards of living and the very way America does business. The very real and systemic problems we face at this confusing juncture of history gives our generation pause.

Given the topsy-turviness of our homes and our society, both during our youth and into the present day, it's no surprise that we are cautiously waiting to sculpt adult lives. We grew up in the wake of a radical decade, an experimental one, and then were whiplashed by one of the most conservative. Now we find ourselves faced with the undeniable signs that our nation is in economic, social, and political turmoil. The rumblings are not going away. We were sired by tradition, nursed on experimentation, and raised in ambiguity. Ambivalence is second nature to the twentysomething generation. It is a survival reflex for us.

Activism — The Boomers Redux

In our generation's rear-view mirror, the Sixties remain a strong reference point. After all, we're the young people of today, and aren't the young people the ones who are supposed to change things? What did that decade of social ferment mean in the larger scheme of things? Does it hold meaning for us in terms of how we should live our lives?

The neoconservatives of the Eighties made fun of the radicals of the Sixties, but many twentysomethings today find themselves respecting the aims of those activists. If you take a good look around, it's hard to ignore what's going on around us. Many of us feel that if you take away the pharmaceutical and sexual excesses, the Sixties were a pretty cool time. But there is an increasing sense of sophistication in terms of how we are approaching social activism. You don't see many unreconstructed hippies around; they are far outnumbered by reconstructed Republicans.

We know now that the environment, resilient as it is, must be protected. We have learned that however you feel about our government's policy of foreign intervention, you should support soldiers who are blamelessly doing their difficult jobs. Much of the opposition to our Middle East policy centered around the slogan, "Support Our Troops, Bring Them Home."

We have vague recollections of the "Great Society" and "War on Poverty" initiatives, yet many wonder why we confront the anguish of homeless people on the street on a daily basis when we provide billions in aid to foreign countries each year. We have those who voted in the Reagan and Bush administrations to thank for such rhetorically appealing, but socially cruel policies. The planet and society really do seem to be getting to a point of no return. Will our generation do anything about it? Will we get another chance if we don't? For those of us who haven't gotten involved yet, maybe it's time to roll up our sleeves and get down to it.

Holding Patterns

Our ambivalence about careers and marriage means that we are not fully participating in life. We may become partial people afraid to live full speed, grow old with grace, and decay with style. We resist complexity, sex, conversation, and tailoring. We insist on maintaining a naif-like pseudo-innocence. The adult world appears perverse, selfish, disenchanted, and full of generalized greed and violence.

Most of us have perfected a stutter-step by now so we can avoid our next stage in life. With so much bizarre turbulence coming from within us and going on around us, it's harder now to reach a stable state of maturity, values, or direction, call it what you will. And it is just these things we need to propel us beyond emotional young adulthood.

Now this may seem obvious, but it's taking us longer to

☐ **Ten favorite holding patterns**

- ■ Unaffected Angst (not the self-consciously hip variety of years past)
- ■ Prolonged, Unfocused Crunchy Granola-dom
- ■ Prolonged, Single-Minded Yuppie Materialism
- ■ Prolonged Sexual Sleaziness (it's cheap at any rate)
- ■ Apathy, Indifference, and Ignorance
- ■ Rationalization (popular since Freud invented it and, I might add, a personal favorite)
- ■ Law School
- ■ The New Age (spiritual steroids)
- ■ Irony
- ■ Resignation (the last frontier)

---

reach an even partially "steady state" because we're asking new questions and delving into areas people never did before at such a young age. How many could've imagined the implications of increased gender flexibility in careers and roles for men and women? How many could've imagine that people could actually physically change their gender?

Who could have predicted the rubble of cracking traditions that lay strewn all around us: divorce, rising political dissatisfaction, social disintegration, a shifting national identity, and wild fluctuations in social and personal values? All these contribute to a more complex series of adjustments that need to be made as we navigate our way through life. And they can eat up a lot of physical, emotional, and spiritual time and energy.

This turbulence—complex, frustrating, and unpredictable as it is—in the last analysis doesn't excuse us from the responsibility we have to get on with it. I have tried to make the point that ambivalence is our natural and understandable reaction to insecure times. Ambivalence, feeling bogged down and confused, all of this is an appropriate response—for awhile. But there may come a time when we become "sick and tired of being sick and tired," when we realize that one must proceed without certainty, when we have to cut our losses and might-have-beens and just do it. Boyfriend x, not boyfriend y. The Southwest, not the East Coast. Computer graphics, not tax law.

Remember you can always alter course once you start, but getting going is the most important thing. This is an exciting and pivotal transformation. We point to new attitudes and directions in our lives and say, "By god, wouldn't you know it, I finally grew up."

THREE

The Transition: Leaving the Beer Kegs Behind

*T*HERE are many things we wish we could know when we leave college. What's it going to be like not having our college friends around to tell us stories and hook us up with dates? How much money do we need to live on? Where should we live? And perhaps most pressingly, what'll it be like not sleeping in?

As we make the transition away from college we need to move on three fronts: getting adjusted to our new environment and making friends, getting a job or at least generating income, and trying to live in harmony with our values.

Suddenly, life gets complicated.

Adjusting to a New Place

At some point we have to jump in and decide where we are going to live after college.

As our college friends split up, many of us are a little stunned by the effects of not having a familiar group of people around. Oftentimes when we move we get so caught up in pounding the pavement in search of a job or getting trained that months may go by before we realize that we haven't made many new friends. This is normal. Most people feel that it takes them about two years to break in socially (shorter if you're in graduate school). We may be working long hours, and our energy feels sapped by the end of the day. We may stop going out as much as we used to. Usually we're too young to relate to many of our older coworkers, although there may be other entry-level people around to hang out with.

The easy sociability of high school and college is gone. People become more private, they start pairing off, there are few if any meeting places where members of a community like college students go and chill. So where can we go when we would like to socialize a little? Where are people stompin' to the Nineties? Bars? Health Clubs? Many of us wind up staying at home, ironing shirts and preparing for tomorrow's schedule.

☐ **Ten Things to Consider When Deciding Where to Go After College**

- ■ Comfortable distance from family?
- ■ Should you move back home?
- ■ Is a particular city about the right size?
- ■ Should you go where you have the best chance of getting a good job?
- ■ Where do you have the most friends?
- ■ What do you need to have a good life? (bodies of water, Indian reservations, nightclubs, mountains, et cetera)
- ■ Should you go to Seattle, Boulder, or Oregon like all the other lemmings, or try some lesser frequented gems like the Twin Cities, Athens, Chicago, or Austin?
- ■ Should you stay in your college town? (correct answer: only if your steady gives you an ultimatum or you have a real job)
- ■ How much is an affordable apartment?
- ■ How much does it cost to triple-dead-bolt it?

It's worthwhile to develop good friendships wherever you go. Not just people you can party with, but people with whom you can really open up. If we haven't met people we are comfortable with, then this is one of our tasks. The trick is, this can be tough even for people who are good at it, who make friends as easily and naturally as the rest of us breathe. How does one go about it?

As with job-hunting, persistence here is crucial. You probably have at least three or four encounters a day when you could make a new friend. Chat with bookstore clerks, secretaries, and street corner musicians. Get to know your neighborhood. Resident barkeeps are often good sources of social information — ask them where all the young people hang out. Don't let promising potential friendships slide. You need all the pals you can get now.

The friendships people treasure most are usually the result of serendipity. They might stem from one of those chance encounters in a class, at work, or through a friend of a friend. Even if you are very personable and open to meeting new people it can take awhile. Plan on about a year or two of feeling peripheral. Move in close to downtown. There you'll find a greater density of people, and thus more potential friends.

Remember: meeting people and making friends is not going to happen if we sit around and wait by the phone. We have to get out, join groups, take a class at the local college, join a club, a church, try out for a play, or whatever. Take up bungee-diving or colonics — anything.

We need support as we make this crucial transition. Many of us consider ourselves lucky if we have a brother or sister or a good friend from way back who makes the time to keep in touch with us. If you feel like you're losing touch with old friends, schedule time for phone calls right into your daily planner.

Try moving into a group housing situation if you feel comfortable with the people there. This can be a good way to reduce isolation. Continue pursuing your old interests in each new place you find yourself. Teach a literacy course, become a Big Brother/Sister; whatever you have done in the past, be it soccer, Spanish, yoga, or whatever, this is the best time to check into local groups centered around your favorite activities. It may seem like a drag to get involved when your schedule is so hectic, but once you start doing it, the chance to get out of your routine will be replenishing.

In her book *The Road from Coorain*, Jill Ker Conway at one point reflects about her family's life in rural Australia. There was a lot of tragedy in their family and her mother became bitter in response, eventually becoming an alcoholic. She didn't really have a group of friends and for whatever reason couldn't say, "Yes, this is terrible and unfair and ruinous, but after you've been down for a while, you have to pick yourself up and get on with it." Friends will help you navigate such crises, provide concrete help, and best of all, make for the good times that we all want to get back to having. Friends can help us avoid a tragic life. Go out and make a million of them.

On The Hunt

Looking for a job is one of the most stressful things you will probably ever have to do. There's no doubt about it. Many people can barely drag out their old resume without a liquid lunch in their bellies first. The best way to proceed is to break down such a major project into small, doable steps.

For those of you who know you want to get a good entry-level job and kick-start your careers, you'll want to put a lot of energy into getting set up and planning ahead. We all know that the world of work is demanding that people be more highly trained and skilled, and that it's taking us longer to become qualified. More professions than ever before now require advanced degrees in order to get off to a good start.

How can fresh college graduates know what they will like and be good at in fifteen years, to say nothing of fifty? The simple answer is, we don't; the trouble is in pretending that we do. Any reasonable expectation of our abilities would leave a lot of room for error, yet somehow we're supposed to be ready for the world, competent and knowledgeable enough to assume full responsibility for that increasingly difficult task. All of the various tidbits of advice and counsel that would be appropriate to this transition to the so-called real world can be summed up in two neat phrases: *know thyself* and *hustle*.

Know Thyself

If you know yourself, then you won't waste a lot of energy running around not knowing yourself. Let's face it. You're twentysomething. You're probably not going to change anything major in your personality now. Little things, maybe. If you've never been a great student, don't run off to grad school in archeology. If you like money, great. Make a ton of it. Do what you have to do. Weave. Fix pipes. Research malnutrition in the Third World. Counsel families in hospices. Program plastic-molding machine-computers to change tools. Work with a studio photographer. To hell with the peanut gallery, and that includes your parents.

A recently married friend discussed with me some of the pals who came to his reception: "Jerry is an old friend from school. Very loyal, kind of stiff, conservative. Hangs out with rich and beautiful people. His investment banking job is perfect for him. He's so happy and excited about it. He's got a heart of gold and he'll always be a treasured friend, even though I'm the kind of person that really needs to have the freedom to work for myself. Let's face it, right now I couldn't go to a meeting that I didn't set up on my own. One of the most valuable mistakes I made was thinking I wanted to go to medical school. It would've been a disaster for me — some doctor calling me up at three in the morning saying, 'get up here, I want you to see this wart.' I probably would tell him that I know what a wart looks like and to screw off and then I'd go back to sleep. It's so much a matter of knowing what you're cut out for and what you're not. And that takes trial and error."

If you're a free spirit, there's no sense kidding yourself about liking finance. You'll make yourself miserable. Instead, feed that free spirit. Get serious about one or several modes of expression. Pour yourself into it.

Knowing yourself is an asset. It takes some folks longer than others, but there are definitely things you can do to accelerate the process. Challenge yourself. Give things the old college try long after college is out. Spend time in foreign cultures. Take different jobs. For example, one guy I interviewed went from wanting to be a windsurfing teacher, to a European history professor, to a psychotherapist, to a speech writer. All of those things contain some aspects of his personality.

I'd guesstimate that for 70 percent of us career hunting is a process of elimination. Maybe 30 percent have a "calling" or join the family firm or something. And even those who are called often want to change at midlife. There is nothing to be ashamed of if you change your mind or decide on something else. The next time you're feeling discouraged about this, think of how many people changed their college major and how many times. It's not that different. Again: ignore the peanut gallery, they'll give you nothing but grief.

A Canadian journalist recalled how his high school French teacher once told him he wasn't "university material" and how he basically resigned himself to being a farmer. He finally took the entrance exams to college, did well, and went on to enjoy his university studies. After freelancing in Germany, France, and Italy he was accepted into a graduate program in Comparative Literature at the Sorbonne in Paris (in English and *French*, he noted with ironic pride).

Are you a person who can motivate yourself? Do you generally feel that bosses are superfluous? If so, great, work for yourself. But if you need someone setting deadlines and teaching you the tricks of the trade, that's great too. Most of us need a balance here, room for some self-direction and some external guidance. Balance it out. Most of us have to deal with a boss whether we like it or not. "Create an atmosphere where the boss knows that she or he is the boss by the way you behave," a friend's father with thirty years of experience at a major automotive corporation advised. "That makes it easier for them to accept you as an employee and team member."

The Paying Your Dues Controversy

It goes something like this. In any field you choose, you have to get your feet wet and do some scut work before you win respect, gain experience, and are prepared to be truly expert at it. This naturally means that you do a lot of the grunt stuff — stuff you may not particularly enjoy — for the higher-ups. All of this, of course, is so that you can be a higher-up someday too, who has young, bright, energetic people like yourself doing the scut work for you.

The pitfall here is being certain that what you are doing is really worth this investment of time and effort. Another person I interviewed disagreed with the conventional wisdom: "I'm basically a hedonist. I believe that if you don't enjoy something, no amount of dues paying is worth it. It's masochism. Why should you break your ass doing something for ten or twelve years just so that you can do more of something you don't enjoy? Look, you've had the privilege of going to college and that means you have choices — what are you doing just settling for anything?"

He's got a point. It's sort of an ends and means thing. If it's really important to you to make partner in an advertising or law firm and that's what turns you on, do what you have to do. If you love the work and you don't care where you end up, try working for someone else for four or five years, get the necessary experience, and make the contacts you need to strike off on your own. People do it all the time. Remember that "paying your dues" is sort of a business deal where you exchange your youth and vigor for intangibles like "training" and "experience." What you get in return varies widely from organization to organization. Supposedly you're being "appropriately exploited" in exchange for experience, contacts, and opportunities for advancement.

Keep in mind that you are not a prisoner here: you can negotiate the terms of your "dues paying." Write your bosses a letter about what your goals and plans for advancement are. Get them to put it on file. See if they're following through with their end of the bargain after awhile. Some people get lucky and get hooked up with a firm that'll pay for European conference trips, or for tuition if they return to school to get their M.B.A. or Ph.D. One man I spoke with even continued getting a full salary on top of free tuition while he did graduate work in mechanical engineering.

It's O.K. to change your mind down the road. Try something for a few years and then reevaluate for yourself whether it's worth it or not. Not everyone makes partner, and too many people waste some of the best years of their life when they could be doing something they like more. So be careful, and remain flexible.

A Hustler's Guide

O.K., brass tacks time. This is all about hustle. Now's the time to get out of the reflective mode and into the active mode. College can make you passive, so be careful. It's not that the pre-meds and engineers are necessarily smarter or more talented than the liberal arts majors. What is true is that they have had regular responsibilities and challenges throughout the last four years and that means they may be more in the "take charge" mode than, say, your average art history major. Remember that student roles are somewhat passive — as in the receiving and regurgitating of information. It's time to get in the driver's seat. The graduation party is over.

If the job market is really bad consider going back to school, but give it at least six months of honest effort first. And by honest effort, I mean putting in at least four hours per weekday in job-hunt related tasks. This is not vacation; don't treat it that way. If you think you'll go broke in that amount of time, get a part-time job and beg your parents for some money to tide you over. Spend it responsibly. Here's how to get started:

☐ Ten Investments To Ease Your Transition Away From College

- A haircut
- A newspaper subscription
- An iron, an ironing board, and the energy to use them
- A good-looking resume and cover letters
- A nice pair of shoes (ever notice how interviewers look at shoes?)
- A credit card and the discipline to use it only in emergencies
- A nice satchel or briefcase, whatever is appropriate for your field
- An organizer with calendar and address book sections
- An answering machine with a professional-sounding message
- A "job-hunt until I drop" attitude

The Transition: Leaving the Beer Kegs Behind

Getting set up/Networking: Let all your friends know you're job hunting. Check with your folks and ask them if they know of any old friends or school buddies in the field you're interested in who might be willing to talk to you. Get them to ask their friends' friends for you. Dig, dig, dig! Follow through with people. Be social; get invited to grown-up parties and weddings. One man reported lining up two interviews and getting the phone numbers of three other contacts at a New Year's Eve party. And he almost didn't go to the party because he was so depressed about not being able to find a job.

You spend half your life learning how to meet people and now's the time to put that knowledge to use. Let yourself be known. The twenties are an excellent time to learn to network, expand your acquaintanceship, and get better at dealing with difficult, aggressive, and pushy people. This ability, in and of itself, is enough for many employers to give you the nod over the competition. Talk to everyone, shop people, pedestrians, Indian chiefs, meditators, mediators, politicians, film critics, and pet owners.

Make friends but keep in mind the following question, particularly for older adults in positions to hear about jobs: "Knowing what I've talked with them about and the way I've behaved in their presence, would they recommend me based on my personal qualifications?" Attention to such detail may make a difference when that dream job becomes available.

Acquire an interview suit/outfit: For men, with few exceptions this should involve a dress shirt, tie, jacket, slacks, and leather dress shoes. For women, some combination of pantsuit or skirt suit is fine, and they have more freedom with colors as well — beige, burgundies, subdued prints and off-white are fine in addition to the traditional blue and gray. Certain work places have idiosyncratic dress norms. Academia tends to be tweedy, nonprofits casual, business, law, and medicine conservative. Try to research the organization you will be interviewing with before the event.

Try to put together two outfits that are interview ready. Iron a spare matching shirt or blouse. This is just in case you spill grape juice on yourself fifteen minutes before you're supposed to leave. This has saved my behind several times before presentations and talks. Some other things to consider doing: have your suit mended or tailored. Shine your shoes. Have your teeth cleaned. Find a lucky charm.

Do some practice interviews with people: Talk to yourself. Practice giving answers to interview questions when you're in the shower or otherwise idle. Read the newspaper and keep up on current events. TV news won't give you nearly the range of opinion or features that a good paper will. Don't get caught not knowing headline news during an interview. Especially don't get caught not knowing about issues that directly relate to your field. Ask for subscriptions to professional and trade journals for gifts from relatives and keep up even if you're not yet employed. One personnel officer in a large computer firm put it plainly: "We don't hire anyone who doesn't seem to know what's going on in the world." Polish up your articulation and try to avoid slang and jargon.

Now you're ready. Job-hunt like a madman: First look in the paper just in case there's anything in the classified section. Then look in the yellow pages under all the possible headings that could have something to do with your field. For instance, if you're going into speech and language pathology, identify all of the hospitals and programs in your community that employ SLP therapists. Contact them by phone and get the name and address of the hiring/firing person. Write them a nice cover letter and send it along with your resume, saying you would like to be considered if any positions are now open or will be opening in the next six months. They should get back to you within a month — if not, call them just to confirm. Job-hunting is all about common sense and being positive and professional. Now, repeat this process over and over again. The interview is actually the last stage in the job-hunting process. The persistent bird gets the worm. If all this begging for work starts getting to you, and it gets to all of us, then do little things to make it easier on yourself. Imagine a friend is helping you accomplish the application process. Bring them along in your mind. Imagine them cracking jokes about a particularly intimidating interviewer during anxious moments.

When you're through with a long hard day of pounding the pavement, do something to burn off that stress: Run or bike or throw the frisbee—do whatever it is you do. Let some time pass. Let your mind glide away from the stress of trying to get hired.

Pat yourself on the back while you make dinner: I don't know anyone who can job hunt without self-esteem. Take care of yourself. It takes a lot of energy to be out there promoting yourself and convincing people to hire you. You might even treat yourself after each *full* day of job-hunting you do. Call a friend or make a milkshake. This is hard work.

Get a good night's sleep: You want to be fresh and energetic for tomorrow and you don't want to look like hell in interviews.

Make your days as normal as possible: Wake up early each day, shower, eat a good breakfast and read the paper at pretty much the same time, hunt all morning, take a lunch break, hunt all afternoon, et cetera, et cetera. In this way you mimic what most work schedules are like. This helps you get into the routine of work before you're even started.

Friendship rules the world: A preexisting friendship between employer and employee guarantees some trust, some fore-knowledge of job skills, and some mutual obligation. Hiring blind offers none of these advantages. But when someone hires a friend without regard for competence or fairness, it's infuriating to the observer. Find it within yourself to respect and use this fact to your advantage instead of feeling bitter about the success of others. Those who say, "all that matters around here for getting promotions is who you know," don't know anybody.

Hard work: The old formula of hard work and persistence is essential to being effective and increasing your skills. Develop a strong work ethic and stick to it. Set goals and check your progress. Don't overlook the basics of getting there on time, maintaining discipline, and warmly contributing to team effort. When you're just starting a new job or launching a career, anxiety and worry are normal. But like Katherine Hepburn said, "When I feel butterflies before a performance, I know it's going to be a good one."

Just pretend: Once you get a job, try not to feel too intimidated at the onset. Everyone is "just pretending" (especially in the beginning) to be a sales rep, a lawyer, a journalist, or a direct care worker. Even very successful people report that they often are amazed that they aren't "found out" for being the frauds that they sometimes feel certain they are. (Your parents were hardly born to the role of parenting. However, they probably did a good job of pretending.) Therefore, be persistent in your pretending, for the skills and assets you develop will be in rough proportion to how much effort you exert.

A lawyer told me that, upon being nominated as a federal judge in Boston, he remembered that whenever court officers referred to him as "Your Honor," he would look over his shoulder to see who they were talking to. He was afraid others in the court might think that there was an impostor on the bench. But as he said, "You finally figure it out. Someone's got to play the role, so I do."

You want your interviewer to think that you're already a

social worker (or whatever), and that you just need a job. You don't want them thinking that you're a person who needs more time to become a social worker first and then find a job to round it out. Be proud of your training! Make sure they know about all of it.

Continuing education: Think of college as the place where you began your education. Strive to continue it by exposing yourself to original thinking, art work, and music. Read, read, read. Newspapers, book reviews, and trade journals will help you keep up with events in your field. I can't emphasize this enough. These can make a difference during job interviews, but they also enrich other areas of your life.

What the Big, Bad World Has in Store

There are lots of super-bright and ambitious people doing annoyingly petty work at the most prestigious law firms and brokerage houses in New York. There are plenty more who have just lost their jobs and are moving back home with mom and dad. The Harvard alumni magazine recently had an article on graduates who have had to take blue-collar jobs.

Things are shifting in the career market place. A lawyer reported only somewhat sarcastically that when he was in college (in the late Fifties) things were different. "My frat brothers never studied, maybe got a 2.2 grade point average, and spent every night at the bar. They didn't know anything about anything but come senior year they would tramp down to the placement office and get a job with U.S. Steel or General Motors. Some of these guys are vice-presidents now. And I tell you I know, because I was there; we got those jobs not knowing how to do much else besides hold a drink and a cigarette in the same hand." How times have

61

changed. Getting some "career moves" down is becoming an increasingly difficult dance step to master.

Alternative Success

There are many ways to make this transition, and much of your decision depends on your values. One group of friends decided to rent a farmhouse and all move in together and live cooperatively after graduation. Their major focus was not so much on starting their careers right away but on enjoying farm life. They started an organic garden, adopted two dogs, and cleaned out an old barn for barn dances and fixing up old cars. They have meadows and woods, a string of visitors, and a very high quality of life.

This is just one example of how your values and priorities make a big difference in terms of determining what to do with your life after college. These people valued community and being able to live close to the land more than going off on their own individual directions in some anonymous mass transit city scene. It works very well for them.

With all the emphasis on careers and being professional these days, it's easy to forget that this kind of choice is still a valid and viable one. What do we really need in order to live? Human warmth, candlelight, a workshop, a garden, good music? You can keep it simple. Several of these "fahmers," as they call themselves, formed a folk group once they moved in together. Most importantly of all, they have time to enjoy each other. They always seem to have some creative project to tinker with.

Questions to ask yourself: do you really need a new car? How important is having a nine-to-five job your parents can tell the neighbors about? What does success mean? "I told my dad after graduation," an editor told me, "not to expect much in the way of big accomplishments out of me during the next few years. The way I looked at it, these years were

☐ Ten Good Job-Hunting Books

After College, by Jack Falvey, Williamson Publishing. Solid advice for pursuing traditional jobs in corporate and other large organizational settings by a seasoned executive.

Jobs for English Majors and Other Smart People, by John L. Munschauer, Peterson's Guides Inc. Written by the Director Emeritus of Cornell University's Career Center.

Graduating to the 9–5 World, by Jerry Bouchard, Impact Publications. Help in getting adjusted to a whole new set of demands and pressures.

Offbeat Careers: A Directory of Unusual Work, by Al Sacharov, Ten Speed Press. Each page offers up an unusual occupation from shepherd to deck hand on a tall ship, along with some information regarding where to find out more.

Guerilla Tactics in the New Job Market, by Tom Jackson, Ten Speed Press. Comprehensive advice from a leading expert and author.

Major Options: A Student Guide to Linking College Majors to Career Opportunities, by Nicholas Basta, HarperCollins. Information that helps you put those next few steps together.

The Resume Catalog: 200 Damn Good Examples, by Yana Parker, Ten Speed Press. Self-explanatory. Check out at least one good resume book. This one's as good a place to start as any.

The Women's Job Search Handbook, by Geri Bloomberg and Margaret Holden, Williamson Publishing Inc. Resource for women and the special challenges they face.

What Color is Your Parachute?, by Richard Bolles, Ten Speed Press. The interest-exploring/job-hunting bible. However, geared more toward the mid-career transition than those just starting out.

The Complete Guide to Environmental Careers, by the CEIP Fund, Island Press. Solid guide to careers in forestry, air, water, and land management.

mine to explore and do with as I saw fit. I just wanted him to know that this was my time and tried to get him to accept that that's what I needed to do with my life at that point."

If you grew up in a community or a family where the only "real" options for adults are to get married and try to get a serious job, think again. If you buy into that kind of mentality you are selling yourself and your life options short. Travel, different living arrangements, the arts and music, mountain biking, all of these things and a thousand more should be available to you. You don't need a million dollars to travel or take some time off from school. But it's certainly helpful to learn the fine art of "the sidejob."

The Sidejob

It's part-time, once in awhile, and usually cash under the table. A very lucrative way to enhance your income. Some examples: dry-wall, cut lawns, help a teacher grade papers, paint houses, stuff envelopes, type, help a busy professional get organized on a project, help set up an art or music show, landscape. The list is endless. The key is getting the word out that you're looking for sidejobs and then keeping up with contacts. Any of the skills you have can be put to use with sidejobs without having to make any huge commitments. That's what's so great about them. Anybody can wait tables for a couple of weeks during the busy part of a restaurant's summer schedule. The key is to keep the gigs coming. Most sidejobs can be done by anyone.

I know several recent college graduates who basically do nothing else but sidejobs and live pretty well. Generally speaking, having a regular full-time job is more advantageous, but some people who haven't had luck finding one do fine with a lot of sidejobs. Flexibility and the willingness to work are all that's needed. Put up some flyers at your local credit union advertising your services. Artists are renowned for having a second steady source of income. One woman was building up a business as a free-lance journalist and made it through the dry months by teaching tennis. It's short, intense work and pays well. That's the ideal kind of sidejob. As for getting started in any kind of free-lance area, she advises taking it one step at a time. "Just tell yourself that you're going to try this for a month and see if you can make any money at it in that amount of time" she advised. "That's how I got started, and one month melted into another, editors kept calling and returning my calls, and before I knew it I had a couple of weekly columns that helped even out the income fluctuations a lot."

Try to avoid the minimum wage route—who wants to have all their time eaten up for so little pay? Another man I spoke with worked as a tutor in the school system and started his own business making screens for cars and vans so people could camp out of their vehicles. He did a tidy little business last year. Again, as long as you're financially self-sufficient, you have the freedom to do as you please. Once you start begging your parents for money, they get to start having a say in what you are or are not doing with your life—a situation to be avoided.

It's important to be practical. Kurt Vonnegut reminds us how few people can really make a living at the arts. He claimed at one point that there are actually more people in this country making their living as admirals in the Navy than there are creative writers making enough money to live on. This is a bit misleading because there are more admirals than you might at first think (between 300 and 400 when you count all the rear, flag, logistics, and intelligence guys), but it is still a startling figure. So, don't give up your day job.

There are great ways to save money by volunteering as well. Can't afford a ticket to your favorite concert? Check out becoming a volunteer usher. "Let's see, this year I saw Laurie Anderson, Jesus Jones, Michael Hedges, and the Pilobolus dance company all free, just for seating people in the balcony," a student friend reported. There are thousands of opportunities like this; you probably don't need as much disposable cash as you might think. Be creative. Check with friends.

Uncommon dilemmas call for creative solutions. You can come up with those solutions if you start thinking outside of the normal channels for getting the things you want out of life. Master the art of the sidejob and you will develop some important skills. Heck, a lot of folks hold a regular job *and* do sidejobs because they want more income. Your time is your own.

Keep Moving

So keep moving on all three fronts of getting a job (or at least generating income), getting adjusted to your new environment and making friends, and trying to live in harmony with your values. Some folks are lucky enough to find all three in one spot — they work and become friendly with people who share their values. Most of us sort of patch it together as we go along. Again, persistence is the key both in developing a social life and job-hunting.

Don't waste your gifts. *Every* person is capable in their own way; some just haven't discovered their gift yet. Some people discover they can write fancy academic treatises or brilliant marketing plans and receive support and encouragement from professors. Others have to bounce around for awhile before they find out where their talent lies. Maybe they have a special talent for fixing things, designing cooling systems, translating, or whatever. The term "gifts" is deceiving, because most people who have certain god-given skills and abilities wouldn't have gotten anywhere without discipline and training. So, don't be afraid of your talents — explore and cultivate them. This is the time in life when we get to figure out what we do and don't want to do.

66

FOUR

Careers and the Long Shadow of the Yuppie Icon

O.K., MAYBE you're not quite ready for the nitty-gritty job hunt yet. Maybe you're still struggling with the question of what you want to do with your life next. Perhaps your career dilemma is at the center of your existence right now, the biggest problem facing you. If so, this chapter is for you. Treating these difficult issues is certainly worthy of a little more attention on my part.

During a long, anxious Michigan winter of confusion about her lack of career direction, a woman I know struck up a conversation with a British fellow at a party. Sensing her self-doubt, he expressed his amazement at how much emphasis Americans put on what people *do*. Where he was from, in Birmingham (northern England), the unemployment rate hovered between 30 and 40 percent. There, placing importance on what people do is a little ridiculous. People were much more curious about what kind of person you are. What are your interests, tastes, politics, and philosophy of life? What sort of sensibilities do you bring to your social circle? What special gifts do you have? Note that all of these questions are relevant to people who don't necessarily have steady work.

This emphasis on the person that she felt coming so strongly from the Englishman helped her to recapture a firm footing of self-esteem. Just because she hadn't conquered the world by the age of twenty-five didn't mean she was worth any less than anyone else. As time went on, this newfound confidence helped to get her out of her funk. Now she's in her second year of medical school.

Often, to be able to accomplish what we desire requires that we grant ourselves the hopefulness to try. She was in a self-defeating cycle: "I haven't done much, which means I won't do much. Why try?" When she was able to say, "Well, maybe I haven't done much, but I'm still a pretty unique individual," she was freed from her shackles.

Given the numerous choices that young people face, how does one go about making some preliminary decisions and narrowing the range of possibilities? Getting out of your confusion about your work future requires that you develop a completely new and different set of skills uncultivated in school. These include expanding your awareness of work options, realistically appraising your own preferences and abilities, learning written and oral professional communication skills, and getting experience related to the field you want to enter. It also requires getting tasks done in the face of sometimes considerable uncertainty and self-doubt.

However, these skills are transferable to the work place you will enter, where you will pursue other projects fraught with uncertainty and self-doubt, (but this time *by noon tomorrow* and *under budget*). The difference is that there you will get paid. That's incentive. How to go about pursuing a career often isn't very well articulated for us. Schools don't teach you how to figure out what to do with your life.

The main thing people need to do when setting out to explore career interests is listen. Think about what sounds intriguing and then go talk to people in those fields. Let them tell stories. Find out how they got started, and what they like and don't like about their job. Ask them what they actually *do* all day. Take a chance. Learn about a career you never considered before. You should keep two goals in mind: get practice asking questions and listening, and gather information — be it through trips to the library, taking notes, attending conferences or workshops, or what have you. What are entry level positions like? What kinds of people work there?

Unfortunately, many people have accepted preordained career or life paths without even being aware that a real choice was made. Dr. Norman Alessi, Professor of Psychiatry at the University of Michigan Medical School, said, "My view of reality is that we always have a lot of choices. Not being aware of them often fouls us up. Some parents subtly or obviously favor business, or psychology or politics, whatever, and their children sometimes wake up at twenty-eight and say, 'Wait a minute! Is this really what I want to be doing?' " There are many choices involved, but that amount of autonomy can be frightening.

Ideology and Practice

Taking time to examine our expectations about the work world is important. Do we expect the infamous "dog-eat-dog" scene, or one in which cooperation and mutual support are prevalent? How flexible do we expect our future employer to be if we have kids and want time off to care for them? Do we expect to make as much money as our parents were able to? Do we expect to be able to buy a house before we're thirty?

It's easy to feel uneasy about the so-called "American Dream." The light and inspiration it affords in giving people hope is crucial. We all benefit from believing that we can improve our circumstances. The American Dream is a compelling legend that has inspired and motivated millions of people to try to stretch beyond their circumstances to build something unique. But the key word here is "legend." There are just barely enough Donald Trumps and Ronald Reagans to keep people believing in the old formulas, even though they don't pan out as often as we'd like to think.

We seldom hear about the people who do their damndest to "make" it by working their whole lives, but for whatever reason never get there. Perhaps they are discriminated against, or the competition is simply too tough, or they just aren't competent enough. We only hear about the heroes. America is full of wasted lives, dashed hopes, and failed aspirations, but it seems impossible to find a place where no one is constantly shoving the unattainable in your face. Coping with failure often demands more heroism from families than does success.

What do we do then? Figure out what works for us and stick with that even if it feels like we're making it up as we go along. A group of alumni who came to speak about careers at a local college suggested that you don't have to know it all ahead of time. They said they spent a lot of years making it up as they went along. Many of them defined some values that they cared deeply about, and then pursued work that supported those commitments. One woman who had been through some difficult experiences with divorce pursued family counseling. Others became journalists and advocates for environmental causes. Others worked for the political asylum of Central American refugees. One even became a first mate for hire on charter sailboats in the Caribbean (harder work than you might think—try varnishing sixty feet of teak trim and a mast all by yourself someday).

As they went about searching for suitable work, they followed their hearts and their noses. Some of them got into trouble; they didn't find the perfect ride. But they did find ways to cope and eventually got themselves out of the bad patches. For the most part, they were content with what they had found.

Getting started in the world is a little like sailing a boat; you can't control the direction of the wind or how fast it blows, but you can set sail, change course, and reduce your chances of capsizing. After we get the hang of it, we learn that it's easier to go in some directions than it is others, that the wind occasionally shifts suddenly, but that we can adjust our course to adjust to change. Eventually, no matter what the conditions, we learn what we need to do to make progress in the general directions we want.

Many of you are probably a little afraid that when you turn sixty-five you might still be confused about what you want to do with your lives. Others of you may be ambitious, directed, and so hardworking that you have forgotten how to play. Still others will have achieved a balance in your lives, but are wondering if what you are doing is best for you.

When you feel the aimlessness blues encroaching upon your good cheer, keep in mind that there are others who probably have lousier jobs than you. I once met a man who used to work on a turkey farm. He did not feed, clean up after, or kill turkeys. Any of you who can come up with a job that is worse than this man's are hereby encouraged to mail it to me at once for inclusion in any future editions of this book. This guy masturbated male turkeys. Later they used the semen for in vitro fertilization. Turkeys followed him around the yard, and the other farm hands called him "turk-jerk," "poultry-puller," and worse. So, whatever you are or aren't doing, just be glad you're not hard up for work and living in the poultry belt.

Stress and Strain

Surveys indicate that an overwhelming majority of men said that keeping a job and making enough money is the toughest thing about being a man in America. One can only imagine how the millions of women feel who can't earn enough to support themselves. The "no experience" resume is considered nearly worthless in many personnel departments. The stress and strain we often experience due to career aimlessness is made worse by pressure from our elders, pressure from a culture that overemphasizes work-related achievement, and pressure we put on ourselves to decide what we want to do with the rest of our lives — precisely when we are least capable of deciding intelligently.

A few strategies for combatting these pressures are: first, quietly tell your elders to piss off (under your breath, that is) and build your own life according to your own principles; second, don't buy into the work-equals-worth equation; third, postpone the "rest of your life" question — as you can hardly have a conversation with yourself at forty, just make plans to do whatever comes next. You can decide later what makes sense for you to pursue after that.

Making work decisions and pounding the pavement in search of a job is difficult. Many people feel chewed up and spit out by the process. One study showed that the average time after graduation before a liberal arts major finds a job in a career area of choice is between eight and ten months. That's a lot of impatience and uncertainty to have to put up with.

Talking it Over

We need a lot of support in these years as we try ourselves out on the world. Don't be afraid to ask for that support. Sometimes after interviewing or an eventful work day, we need to talk over how we responded to interviewers or coworkers as we try to learn about office dynamics. Try to find good listeners who have some work experience. Find a mentor in your field, or just someone who shares your interests. They can help you see the bigger picture and ask you the kind of questions you need to be asked to be able to go on to your next step.

One common mistake is overpersonalizing work place dynamics (i.e. shouldering too much of the blame for projects run amok) because of the desire to do a perfect job. One lab assistant who was studying to be a scientist began to feel more and more ambiguous about her job because the data that she was coming up with wasn't what the principal investigators (her bosses) were looking for. After talking it over with a friend she realized that her job was just to perform the experiments to the best of her ability and that she really had no control over how the data came out. This helped her detach herself from whatever the desirability of the data was and made her a more objective scientist.

Mission Possible

Making even tentative career choices can be trying, especially if you're an original. If we don't seem to operate along the lines that the world has laid out it's easy to get discouraged. What you have to do is find something that suits your individualistic needs and desires. One poet friend talks about how everyone else is trying to develop their "responsibility," whereas he, as a poet, needs to cultivate his ability to go into a contemplative state of "repose." He tries to develop his "repose-ability," although after six months or so, one of his employers lost tolerance for his daydreaming ways and started dropping hints that he should "shop around." Poetry doesn't pay well, but what poets do — contemplate and explore the inner life — is very important.

One usually has to make some sacrifices and compromises as we seek the work we aspire to perform. But that shouldn't stop you from going full steam ahead. This is your chance to dream up something that you have a strong interest in and pursue it. If you love something, do it and keep it close by. Learn what makes you happy and go for that. Many of us will discover what it is we want to do in this way, but not all. For some of us it's more a matter of giving up the hope

for the perfect job and getting on with its closest approxima-
tion. Remember, the world is not obligated to pay you to do
exactly what you want to do. But it might if you're lucky.

Some people look for a "mission" like AIDS education or
protecting children from abusive parents. This can be an excellent way to proceed. Sometimes the most noble and socially redeeming work is done by those who think carefully
about what types of careers are worthy of pursuit. It's important to be forthright with yourself about your values, because you begin to feel very kindly towards whoever is sign-
ing your paycheck.

One man I spoke with went to law school during the Vietnam War, and his indignation about what was happening
led him to establish a nonprofit legal counseling foundation
for military personnel subjected to military injustice. In addition to his legal work, he has become involved in researching and writing books about Agent Orange and defending
people who lost their jobs due to their sexual orientation or
as a result of blowing the whistle on illegal military activities. He is a good example of how someone can let their
values structure their life work. Do not, however, wait
around passively for a mission to fall in your lap. Explore
one or two that might tap your skills and energies.

Parents

"If you only knew," a seasoned therapist related, "how many
doctors and lawyers I see in my practice who finish their
training and two years into their jobs realize they hate it and
that they are only doing it for their parents." Several therapist acquaintances of mine have remarked on how often
they see clients living out their parents' ambitions and not
their own.

Unfortunately, this is a big problem. Pitched battles can
go on for years over what you are or are not doing with your

life. Values, money, time spent, what kind of person it's making you, all of these things cut to the core of where a family stands on what's truly important in life. Our parents have dreams for us. A seasoned family therapist on the brink of retirement once said, "all kids disappoint their parents, otherwise they wouldn't be human."

There is a metaphysical accounting system at work in families. We "owe" parents certain things in a psychological sense because they brought us into the world. Our guilt and sense of obligation to our parents is a big issue in our twenties. With so many two-career families, for instance, you get loyalty dilemmas. "If I go into career counseling like my mom, won't dad be slighted a little that I didn't join him in the shop?" a senior at the University of Michigan asked me. And he was right; he later called to tell me that his father took him aside and gave him a special invitation to come back to the shop anytime, even if he tried something else first. This pressure and others are often at work. Some families feel that no serious work is really done outside a major corporation.

These dynamics can give young adults complexes. Many of us try to do what they want us to do in an effort to make our parents proud and happy. Unfortunately, this isn't a very reliable approach to contentment for either party. Some parents like the sound of "my daughter the doctor," or "my son the vice president" just a little too much for our well-being. Keep in mind that you may only be mediocre at something your parents want you to do, but you might be brilliant at something they don't want you to do. Just ask the cellist Yo-Yo Ma, whose parents pushed him toward science and medicine.

Conversely, class pressures can work in the opposite direction. A psychologist who sees a lot of graduate students observed that many of her clients who come from lower-income backgrounds struggle the most at the very end of their dissertation work. She calls them her "ABD" clients. In academia-ese this means you have finished all your course work and are All But Dissertation, but to her this means Anything But Disloyalty. She works with these students to try to identify how their fear of finishing their Ph.D. might grow out of a desire to avoid being "disloyal" to their working-class parents. This anxiety robs them of energy to push on and get it done. They fear their parents will think they are snobs.

The Yuppie Icon

So you don't happen to have investment portfolios, advanced degrees, and trendy condominiums? Don't be so intimidated. As it turns out, yuppies only make up four million of the estimated 72 million baby-boomers. Although they are far less visible in the media, there is a huge community of people who are twentysomething, floundering, and off the yuppie track. Instead, they have been off cultivating creative pursuits, putting energy into their communities, and paying close attention to their family bonds. Thank goodness.

In the status-conscious Eighties it seemed like everyone was printing up business cards describing themselves as some sort of "consultant." Title inflation reduced professional currencies. Salespeople became "account executives," secretaries "administrative assistants," insurance salesman "brokers," and companies of four were made up of one president and three vice presidents (all of whom answered the phones). One of my interviewees had a travel agent whose card read, "Travel Engineer." The guy who walks across the yard spreading pesticide on your grass is called by his company, without a trace of irony, a "*field* specialist." This is a rather pathetic reflection on our national insecurities.

Being in your twenties used to mean coming to grips with confusion, self-definition, and painful choices. In the early

Seventies, according to a group that studies trends in higher education, "developing a meaningful philosophy of life" was the number-one life-goal of incoming college freshman. By 1989 it had dropped to ninth, and the number-one life-goal was "being well-off financially." Fewer people are using higher education to find out who they are, who they ought to be, and what is worth knowing. We're going to need a lot more maturity to make it into the next millenium as a society.

Underachiever and Proud of It!

Despite the suffocating overemphasis on "success," there are some signs in popular culture that there are people striving to redress the balance. Bart Simpson, the irreverent *enfant terrible* of "The Simpsons" TV show, burst onto the national stage emblazoned across an infamous T-shirt proclaiming, "Underachiever and Proud of It!" The virulent response from community leaders everywhere was an indication of what a raw nerve he hit. School principals across the nation demanded the removal of this T-shirt from stores, arguing that it reinforced an already poor attitude among youngsters.

There is an exuberant, healthy streak a mile wide in Bart's "Emancipation Proclamation." Not every kid, regardless of how hard he tries, is going to be a big achiever. Sure, kids out there need to be encouraged to develop a wholesome discipline appropriate to their age, but I would sleep better knowing that they are less pressured about achievement. One interviewee's favorite T-shirt from his Sixties days read, "Nurture Your Kid, Go Fly a Kite." In other words, leave them be.

An acquaintance of mine is becoming a clinical psychologist and his area of interest is suicide in young children. And I'm not talking about twelve-year-olds here—try six- and

eight-year-olds. There is a significant number of such sui-
cides, and the occurrence of these truly terrifying acts is rising. How much stock can one put in a civilization where
some of its youngest members, barely old enough to ride a
bike or climb a tree, have the anguish and the conviction and
the wherewithal to do away with themselves?

In my view, the most successful kids are the ones who
learn how to feel good about themselves and how to make
others feel good. How many *adults* do you know who have
learned these skills? This is far more important to the better-
ment of our society than a bunch of overachieving, emotional wrecks who have had the Harvard insignia projected
on to their brain stem from their first few months in the
womb.

Pessimism is Unpatriotic

Eugene Debs Hartke, the protagonist of Kurt Vonnegut's
Hocus Pocus, is a college teacher who is fired on the grounds
that he is "too pessimistic." The administration argues that
pessimism is as unpatriotic as socialism. In as un-American
a fashion as one could imagine, Hartke explains, "I see no
harm in telling young people to prepare for failure rather
than success, since failure is the main thing that is going to
happen to them." I find this heartening. I wish there were
more cultural messages out there that dealt with failure beyond the old cliche, "you win some, you lose some."

I can't stress these points enough. Many of us have known
failure already, or will soon. Failing once in awhile means
that we are taking risks and stretching ourselves. We need to
learn to experience failure safely so that we can learn to get
on with it, to regroup, and to recognize our humility as ordinary, fallible human beings. The wisdom that comes with
age probably has more to do with greater experience of failure than with greater experience of success.

One highly successful business tycoon provided a different perspective on how failure works in the grander scheme of things. In his circles, failure is positively a requirement for admission. When an elite organization is looking for investors he reports that most will only accept you if you, as he puts it, "can be dribbled." What that means is that other investors are more attracted to a project if they know that the people in charge can "bounce," that they've made and lost and remade their fortune, often many times over. This means that they can hack the bad times and break through the depression and ennui that is such a part of business failure and get themselves going again. In their minds, evidence that you can bounce back from failure is practically an occupational requirement.

Don't waste your energy trying to appear ideal. Instead, wear a little of your failure on your sleeve. Flaunt it in the face of the "success prudes" around you. This is one way we can begin to make our culture a little more sane. Brag about how you bounced back; you deserve it. Our culture fails to recognize the vast majority who hove-to in the middle ground of only partial success.

There is a lot to learn on the ladder down that can help you climb back up once you're over the initial shock. Of course, failure hurts. It can make us feel worthless and incompetent. Few experiences feel worse on the job, in a relationship, or with family and friends. After we get over that initial shock, however, the path out of it usually becomes clearer. There is no genuine self-expansion without failure.

Fishing for Careers

Planning the first steps of your career is a little like fishing. When are the best times for you to fish? What kind of lures or bait might you try? How deep do you set your bobber? And where are the best holes? Where do the big ones hang out? Or are you more comfortable with the smaller fish that don't strain you so much when you reel them in? These things are probably worth exploring before you go casting wildly around, scaring all the fish (but hooking mainly old tires).

One of the best guides available to help you with this is Richard Bolles' book *What Color is Your Parachute?* (see chapter three). Bolles emphasizes that there are things you can be doing during your "fishing expedition" to improve your competence in "transferable skills." These skills include: organizational abilities, diplomacy, initiative and the ability to take charge, writing skills, creativity and brainstorming powers, and powers of observation. Even if you're not employed, consider your exploration and development of these related skills as a part-time job and spend your remaining time looking for internships or work.

Taking Charge

Learning how to take charge is fundamental to getting a good job and having an exciting career. You will also find it wins you respect and rewards in many other areas of your life as long as you use it appropriately and sparingly.

By taking charge, I don't mean dominating others. Rather, be in control of yourself and don't do stupid things when your competence is on the line. Take a time management course. Sounds corny? Wrong. Know what needs to happen, be sure you secure the resources to accomplish it, and get it done. This is a tricky nexus of skills and abilities to untangle, but learning to take charge is very related to: knowing what you want; knowing how to get it; letting key people and institutions know in persuasive ways why you deserve it or how you will pay for it; and becoming politely assertive in such a way that wheels turn.

If you learn any one of these skills you are on the road to

developing the whole set. These are the attributes of a capable person with high self-esteem, someone we would all like to resemble a little more. Learn to associate pleasure with what you want to accomplish and pain with whatever is holding you back. Try making some minute changes today in how you approach your work or search for work; tomorrow, maintain the changes you've effected and add a few more small goals. Pretty soon you'll realize how strongly we are conditioned to avoid projects that aren't in reality that difficult. We make them so only in our minds.

Zen and the Art of Photocopying

Young people are often discriminated against when they first take a job. We get knocked for being "green," "wet behind the ears," and unreliable. You can fight this by dressing appropriately at work functions, polishing your polite social skills, and getting better at being deferential. Know your forks. Make sure, with each gesture, utterance, memo, and phone call that your boss knows that you know who's the boss.

Believe it or not, the older people we work with appreciate us for the spice we bring to their mornings. Nothing quite makes their day like seeing us half-swaggering, half-dragging our way into work in the same clothes, nursing a hangover and recounting tales of the hottest new nightclubs around town. They need to know that some people are still young enough to go on midnight Vegas runs, to sneak into hotel hot tubs for a rendezvous, and to dance all night long and still be able to talk at work the next day (an ability I am sadly losing).

People in their twenties often start off in stressful jobs. Dealing with irate customers, putting out fires, deflecting subtle and not-so-subtle sexual harassment — the list is long. Unfortunately, at this time in our lives we are at our most vulnerable and unsure as to how to handle these things. Being low on the totem pole gets old pretty quick. Keep in mind, however, that there is a lot to be said for learning the basics of whatever business you're in from the bottom up. Better that you suffer a little now and become a skilled and fair boss later than to try to supervise people with whose work you are completely unfamiliar. On the other hand, you can only stand so much time at the copy machine.

Internship

If you're not sure how to proceed, do some research and check into an internship. Our nation's capital is chock full of them. One man told me the story of his dissatisfaction with his graduate training in the field of organizational psychology. After the first few years of highly theoretical academic work he decided he wanted to find out what real people were doing in the community. He approached a psychologist about whose work he had heard good things and offered him a proposition. If he was allowed to observe him working with a client once a month, he would write up everything he saw and try to mesh it with the theories and research topics that he was exposed to in graduate school. The psychologist agreed.

The student took a lot of time preparing his write-up of what he observed because he wanted very much for it to be worth his trainer's while. As time went on, the trainer found this process extremely valuable. Another set of fresh, curious eyes and an eager imagination helped illuminate his practice for him. Soon, other students in the department got in on the act. This mentoring relationship grew over the years into a friendship that still endures. Now the trainee runs a successful consulting business modeled on his mentor's practice.

Interning is a very effective way to become visible in a field, learn a little about it, and have a name to drop when applying elsewhere. Don't let your age or inexperience stop you from exploring.

Gender and the Work Place

Beginning at a young age, women are subjected to a mixed series of rewards and punishments for being assertive, competent, and knowledgeable. This often discourages them from pursuing ambitious goals. If you are the first in your family to pursue a career (as opposed to working at home) you may suffer from the absence of role models, as well as sexual harassment and discrimination. In many ways your situation resembles that of first-generation college students, except that you don't "graduate" for forty years. One female I interviewed is an equal partner in a consulting team made up of three social workers. Whenever they go to a hotel to give a presentation the hotel managers begin to address her male colleagues as "Doctor," and turn to them to make any important decisions, while treating her without the same sort of deference. This is just a small example of how implicit sexist values gum things up.

As more women achieve professional success in the work place, they will begin to learn what men have known all along: professional success, important as it is, doesn't necessarily have much to do with how good you feel about yourself. Men often have the advantage of an early indoctrination in sports, which enables them to see careers as like a game. Thus we play the "game," "win some and lose some," and sometimes recognize that "look, it's just a game!" Several of the women I interviewed, when asked, "what one thing would you change about your work?" reported, "I would learn to become less emotionally involved with what happens there."

Many men, expecting pressure from women in their personal lives to be successful, are surprised by pressure to develop their interpersonal and "soft" sides. This combination is often overwhelming. Due to the pressure to be the efficient, take-charge kind of guy at work, and then to come home and suddenly become more sensitive and interpersonally astute, many men walk around feeling confused.

There is probably some truth to the assertion that if we were all *really* in touch with our feelings a lot of the world's work probably wouldn't get done. Sometimes we need to be ruthless. There is a balance to strike here. As Eleanor Roosevelt said, "Most of the work done in the world is accomplished by someone who wasn't feeling well that day."

The Department of Belabored Statistics

If you're unsure about what you want to do, be wary of government sources. The Department of Labor's statistical report is hardly inspiring. It reports that future openings will be in information processing, telecommunications, service industries, and computers—perhaps not necessarily what you had in mind. But be creative and look around you. The department is hardly going to announce, "By 1997 there will be a shortage of tenor sax players, virtual-reality amusement park entrepreneurs, and wax museum curators."

One interviewee reported that after checking into a job at a brokerage house in New York, he decided to go to Hungary. He quickly found work with a consulting firm that helps Western organizations trying to get a start there. Not long ago he accompanied a client to the Hungarian Parliament, where he helped present proposals regarding potential locations and tax incentives for this client's enterprise. At twenty-six he's doing what his peers back in New York would only get a shot at if and when they've "made partner," and probably not even then. This is a good example of creative, unconventional, and unyuppified career pursuit.

The Art of Creating Options

Given a swiftly changing corporate environment, the one-company career is more myth than reality. There is no security in assuming that things will move in a linear direction for you from here on out. They won't. The major finding from my interviews regarding career paths is how atypical and unpredictable they are. People flip back and forth between all kinds of different fields, using completely different skills. Unfortunately, many people mutter about these developments under their breath. It's as if we should all maintain the illusion that there is one career path to a person's life, that one company is enough. This is patently ridiculous and those in a position to counsel us would do us a favor if they would admit it.

One man's career path went like this: he majored in psychology at the University of Michigan, then went to New York and drove a cab in Manhattan. After that, he went out west and became a direct care worker at a juvenile treatment center and took classes to become a music therapist. After he got his certification he worked at Napa State (psychiatric) Hospital for about three years. At this point he got sick of mental health work and joined an acting troupe that toured around northern California. Then he became a busboy, formed a band, taught guitar lessons, and finally wound up going to Japan for four years to teach English. Eventually he returned to the University of Michigan as a graduate student in Japanese literature, got a master's in that, and then switched to the School of Social Work and got his master's there. Now he is finishing his Ph.D. in developmental psychology focusing on cross-cultural studies of education and development in Asia. He's the kind of person who should be a career counselor, and I'm sure many of his future students will take advantage of the resources he has to offer.

The refreshing thing about interviewing this man was

that he wasn't at all bashful about his quitting a "middle-class" job to take a job in a restaurant as a busboy. "Hey," he said, "sometimes you need a change, and if you fear for your well-being then take something else, anything." Many people experience this. Basically my message is this: exploring a variety of jobs is O.K. in your twenties. It's still discovery, even if you're learning more about what you *don't* want to be doing.

One can very rapidly go from a seemingly secure, steady $40,000-a-year job to part-time work at the local bookstore or restaurant. Unexpected things happen. They originate from both outside and inside forces. Where your security lies is in building confidence and skills in your ability to anticipate, adapt, and restructure your circumstances according to the vagaries of the work world. This is the art of creating options and keeping them open. Network carefully. Despite the overconfident assertions of forecasters and futurists, nobody really knows how things will wash in the economy over the next several years. Prepare for this by expecting unpredictability.

Waking Up from the American Dream

The excessive hope inherent in the American Dream has been and will increasingly become a major source of social frustration. The self-loathing and the strong sense of personal failure in those who are let down are a product of the hope dangled in front of them. Telling people that they can be, have, and do *anything* is cruel.

In reality, this promise is far from the truth. If you take a minute to think about it, it's ridiculous to tell people they can become anything they want to. Talk to a manager in any organization; there are very real limits to what certain people can and cannot do. Many of the people who don't become whatever they want to be may begin to see themselves as failures, or as somehow lacking in moral character, when this is hardly the case. The system presents limits (and opportunities) as do individuals themselves, and it is in this submerged collision that our fates our wrought — *not* in fulfilling our end of some simplistic formula for success. Obviously, economic outcomes are determined by innumerable factors, of which following the naive formulas prescribed to us in the ideology of the American Dream is one of the weakest. We would do well to keep in mind a more critical, complex, and skeptical mindset regarding success.

These social ideologies that "you can be anything you want in America" and "have it all" are misleading and destructive to young people. The media makes the prospect of having a dual-income family with kids seem like a merry adventure that organized and enthusiastic people can meet with grace and charm. Well, take a look around. Families are being systematically deprived of their most valuable resource: time. Something has to give, and the anomie and alienation of young people in America is testament enough to what is giving. Kids suffer when they cannot interact with adults on a regular basis.

The portrayal of the dual-income family with kids as a bracing challenge smilingly met by winning parents is an icon of our times. It can make people who don't want to embark on such a dubious lifestyle feel like they are less than adequate. Our economic system feeds itself on people who buy into the ideology that is constantly bombarding us: *strive, strive, strive* for *more, more, more,* and *have it all.*

Having two such full-time roles poses a lot of questions that cut to the core of our lives. Primarily, it poses the question of integration. How does an individual who is expected to play more than one role balance the clashes, inconsistencies, and stresses in their lives and still remain intact? This is a question that deserves further exploration and study and I can think of no better starting point than Perri Klass's book *Other Women's Children.* She is a Boston-based pediatrician whose writing explores these issues in poignant and hilarious detail.

In any case, economic pressures to live well are resulting in nothing less than the emotional neglect of millions of children. It's not the parents who are to blame but a complex set of social and economic circumstances. There is no rationalizing a world that demands insane commitments from parents and renders them incapable of spending time with their kids. The members of the twentysomething generation will probably also be "sandwich" caretakers too, having to care for both our parents and our children simultaneously. And this is to say nothing of larger questions about our economic system. What can a society and a family sanely bear? How we balance these forces in our lives is becoming the crucial challenge of the Nineties.

Everyday Heroism

One minister told me of how, as time goes on, he is more and more moved by the heroism of everyday people barely managing to hold their lives together. Although the scale is much smaller, the modest victories of some of his parishioners are no less glorious than the accomplishments of Winston Churchill. And once we feel we've reached some sort of balance, it requires constant adjustment. Peggy Noonan, formerly Ronald Reagan's speechwriter, said it well: "Most people don't feel appreciated enough, and the bravest things we do in our lives are usually known only to ourselves."

At any rate, there are a lot of contradictions and challenges that we as a generation will have to face in the years to come. These are intimidating problems in that it's hard to imagine a way to lessen the economic demands placed on us. Many of us swear in the same breath that we will spend a lot of time with our children and that we will have it all in terms of material things. This ideology is on a collision course with life.

The good news is that we do get to have some choice in what we want to pursue. Financial security should take care of itself down the line. Pursue happiness first. If you are doing what you want, you may easily come upon ways to make money doing it. But you'll never notice these opportunities until you've made the commitment to pursue that ideal.

FIVE

Activism

WE KNOW that the world is far from being a perfect place. The oppression of women, children, minority groups, the mentally ill, animals, and the homeless that we see around us is unacceptable. Many of the dictatorial regimes currently in power in countries around the world are equally unacceptable. The world bombards us with images of the good life that beckon us to expend more energy on commercial fantasies than on real people. How can we avoid the "We're doomed, so let's party!" attitude? What can we do to improve the world and lead rewarding, responsible lives, and skirt the typical twentysomething pitfalls in doing so?

Flash-in-the-Pan Activism

Because you are either wise enough or far enough away from college, you know that saving the world generally doesn't feed the bulldog. Blanket activism without realistic, attainable ends is a formula for burnout and breakdown. Many people have found very real and important work that needs to be done ecologically, socially, and internationally. Activism is crucial. But basic responsible living can't be avoided by rationalizations about "greater causes."

Despite descriptions in the media of our "apathetic" tendencies, our generation does feel strongly about the severe problems we see around us. We're just not calling as much attention to ourselves as we go about heightening our awareness and getting involved. As one man from Texas said, "I get sick of activists who are 'all hat and no cattle'." Many people feel that they would like to do something but aren't quite sure how to proceed. Some question how making an intense (and often low-paying) commitment will mesh with their other goals like travelling, going back to school, or having a family.

"Flash-in-the-pan" activism is an all-too-common scenario. Many volunteer organizations see lots of people at their first organizing meetings and recruitment drives, then watch their recruits dwindle when the real work starts. Commitment involves time, work, and frustration. It's natural that some folks drop out. One volunteer coordinator reflected, "I hate to say it, but some of our best volunteers are the ones fulfilling a community-service obligation for a judge. They show up the most consistently and are the most reliable. And it's all because they need a letter from us saying they did the work to our satisfaction." On the other hand, it is estimated that one in two adults in the U.S. volunteers at least five hours a week, and we are one of the few nations with so high a percentage. This is an incredible number of people who are daily exerting a remarkable amount of effort in their communities. Many report that job anxieties, personal worries, and negative outlooks slide right off your back when you volunteer.

One activist from the Southwest speaks about how important it is for him to see his activism sustained over the long haul. Many of his younger colleagues tended to display the aforementioned flash-in-the-pan activism. They would be totally gung-ho as they embarked on their first activist responsibilities and would often burn out in eight months or a year. Too often they became cynical, stopped acting on their (previously passionately held) values, and basically just lapsed into a "paying the bills" mentality. To him, figuring out ways to sustain his commitment is critical.

Avoiding the flash-in-the-pan syndrome requires some reining in. It means avoiding eighty-hour weeks. It means taking vacations and figuring out ways to let the other parts of you get a chance for expression. Strike a bargain with those parts of you that want to travel. Work in a different field for awhile. Pacing and balance will allow you to keep making a contribution, however humble, well into your thirties and beyond. Just because you bump up against some bureaucratic walls and begin to see that the world doesn't change as quickly as you would like it to doesn't mean your efforts are worthless. And it doesn't mean you'd necessarily be better off going back and joining the family firm. Unfortunately, disillusionment and frustration are parts of activist work that cannot be avoided, just as they are aspects of work in every field.

Maslow's Bellyflop

Many, though not all, twentysomethings have perfected this difficult diving maneuver. Leaping off the springboard of college, we aim for a life of ideal proportions. Reaching ever upwards in flawless poise, our bodies ripple with grace. Almost imperceptibly, though, at the height of our extension, something goes awry. We begin to lose control, tip off balance, and suddenly find ourselves crashing down belly-first in a messy splash of tangled limbs, muffled groans, and far-flung spray. Now we have to tread water for dear life.

When we "launch" ourselves from college into the world (which in my case was more like a sputtering away), we're long on idealism and short on practical knowledge. We quickly begin to learn that what is meaningful for us doesn't necessarily translate into salaried work. We may lose some of the hope and passion that previously fueled our furious pace. Some of us abandon our professed values altogether.

The well-known psychologist Abraham Maslow is perhaps most famous for his theoretical model known as Maslow's Hierarchy of Needs, which he conceptualized as a pyramid made up of ascending levels. At the bottom are simple survival needs like food, water, and shelter. When these are secured, we can "move up" to the next level of social needs, such as belonging to a group and fulfilling roles within that group. When these are met, we can move on to the ego's need for recognition, respect, and distinction as a result of our efforts and labors. Then we try to fulfill our emotional needs, and so on. As we reach the apex of the pyramid, we reach for self-actualization in previously unexplored potentials. At this peak we aim for personal realization, or what is also called fulfilling our potential, life's mission, or making a contribution.

The diving metaphor above describes the path that many twentysomething people take. We often leave college aiming to fulfill ourselves and change the world in one bold stroke. We have yet to develop realistic notions of the time real change requires, and a correspondingly appropriate humility. For example: a student in profound engagement with his religious heritage goes to Israel and decides to become a rabbi so that he can facilitate religious exploration in other people. Another student, fresh from the healing she experienced after her own personal therapy, decides to become a counselor so that she too can catalyze healing in others.

Maslow would say that when we've bellyflopped into our adulthood, we have plunged from seeking out our self-actualization needs to worrying about our basic security needs. This occurs when the would-be rabbi inevitably questions the realism of his personal motives and spiritual goals, and when the counselor doubts her impact and weighs the stress that comes with it. The rabbi-in-training, after the failure of one of his own relationships, wonders how he will counsel older people who come to him with relationship concerns. His lack of confidence grows so great he considers dropping out. The counselor's first job is working at a school for the "developmentally disturbed," which she soon realizes is a euphemism for student-thugs. Male students sexually proposition her and the girls in her class daily. The whole school exists in a state of siege. Kids bring knives and guns to school, have no textbooks or even chalk to use, and even the principal admits that the school has little to offer beyond glorified babysitting. If her disillusionment grows strong enough, she will wind up leaving her job. If and when this happens, one suddenly faces the question of where the money will come from next.

Such a rapid shift of the "need" levels to which we are attending can be disorienting and stressful, and turns our graceful swan-dive into adulthood into a tangled bellyflop. Whether we call it an "identity crisis," a "career-confusion crisis," or a "spiritual crisis," it can be hard to come to terms with, largely because our culture teaches us to invest so much of our identities in our work. When Americans ask each other "what do you do?" we generally respond by saying, "I am a carpenter," instead of "I do carpentry."

There are other pitfalls to beware of, such as allowing your ideals to become so rigid that they prevent you from functioning responsibly. An extreme example of principled inflexibility could be seen in the case of a not-so-recently graduated friend who became involved with revolutionary politics. He refuses to take any job that involves buying or selling, a hierarchical worker-manager relationship, or in any way smacks of "the establishment." He's now living at home with some very irritated parents and has no job prospects.

The puncturing of your youthful idealism doesn't necessarily have to lead you to apply for a position at Merrill Lynch. Let's just remember that it's important to establish self-sufficiency in addition to attending marches, protests, and candlelight vigils. It's much easier to respect what people say about the injustices of the world when they're supporting themselves.

In many ways disillusionment is a necessary rite of passage for idealistic young people. That first idealistic fervor launches us out into the world with enthusiasm and propels us through our first few jobs or causes. But its eventual cooling allows us to make healthier, more realistic choices about our futures.

A woman I spoke with became a VISTA volunteer after she developed strong concern for the homeless while in college. After six months of work, she realized that her city's programs were aimed more at making the homeless invisible than doing anything substantial to help them. Much of her job involved setting up a transportation network to take homeless people to an inadequate out-of-town shelter. She felt betrayed by the people who hired her and by the community's attitude toward the homeless. She isn't sure what she would like to do with her life now and has to drag herself to work everyday. Anticipate some disillusionment during your initiation to activism. Forewarned is forearmed.

Burnout is another potential mine field. It exists everywhere and not just in the helping professions, although the kinds of burnout people experience in human service jobs can cut to the spiritual core. A family therapist I interviewed still has nightmares about the gun a father pulled on him during a family session three years ago. Business burnout is more likely to be due to boredom or feeling overwhelmed by overwork. But these people are often rewarded with bonuses and commissions, which are seldom available to those in the helping professions.

The Twin Faces of Activism

It is hard to steer between the two sides of the American psyche. One side says that it's important to speak out against injustice and exploitation. If you went to college, you were repeatedly reinforced in this behavior. On the other side, loyalty to the interests of the group — any group — is supposedly of tantamount value. Right after college, many people get caught over the great chasm between these two positions. To "join the system" is to be part of the problem, but to find a good job in "politically correct" arenas has its challenges and frustrations as well. If our activism is motivated mostly by guilt we are headed for trouble, because one can never do enough to eradicate the injustices around us. A little guilt is natural, but people need to work for something positive within themselves if their experiences are to be positive ones.

One friend who worked for the Public Interest Research Groups (PIRG), which fight corporations in an effort to make them more socially and environmentally responsible, reported that he often had conflicts with his regional supervisor. She wanted to run the organization more like a corporation, complete with standard regional policies, quotas, and so on. If employees didn't make their fundraising quotas she tried to get rid of them. My friend fought this because he valued the unquantifiable "conversion" efforts of these people as well as their fundraising achievements. What if they recruited volunteers? What if these recruits started giving their congressmen hell and helped organize protests? He felt his supervisor's policy meant that these people were treated like so many salesman who have to make commission or they're fired. Ultimately he left to work for a more collectively run organization in New York, although he does respect PIRG's concrete achievements.

Not all activist experiences will be so complex, however. After getting her degree in psychology, a woman I talked to who had worked at Planned Parenthood and in other health clinics set up in Los Angeles, where she had heard about a unique new program. She was hired as a community educator by a public health agency. Basically, when her clinic finds people who test positive for HIV, they are asked to list all of their previous partners. She then goes out into the community and tracks those people down to inform them and encourage them to get tested. Her territory is in rugged East

L.A., and she mostly deals with gang members. It's tough, tiring work, and she has seen her share of guns and violence. They have her pegged as a "white liberal middle-class girl from the suburbs," and they're right, but she doesn't let that stop her.

Hardhats for Hardheads

Our generation is perhaps a bit more hardheaded about activism than those who came of age in the late Sixties. We try to be practical and results-oriented in our approaches. We would rather work slowly and steadily than take an intense stance only to abandon it later, as portrayed among the characters in *The Big Chill*. If you saw the film, you might remember the soliloquy by the woman who went to law school in order to help the underprivileged, but eventually went to work for a corporation. Again, teasing out how much of this image is a product of the media and how often it really occurs is difficult. As one man told me: "In April of 1988 I went to the twenty-year anniversary of the Columbia University student rebellion. They had panels and presentations with the basic theme of activists at midlife: 'Where we were then, Where we are now, Where we are going. . . ' The one thing that struck me deepest was how all these hundreds of people still held the values and political convictions of those formative years — and in whatever way many of them were still political — as teachers, social workers, or counselors. They had evolved and grown but they had not abandoned their basic beliefs and goals."

It takes time for realistic expectations to emerge. Certainly, in cases like the environmental situation, we know some of the directions we need to take. However, it would obviously be an unmitigated disaster to leave, say, the disentangling of the arms race to a bunch of well-meaning college students.

Among my college cohorts (class of 1986) the desire to forego riches in order to join a helping profession was considered a noble example of "taking the high road." I bumped rather rudely into my ego when I fully appreciated the salvation fantasy that lies behind much of psychotherapy. Some clients just didn't get better. Through whatever combination of my own lack of experience, their lack of will, or troubling circumstances, some got worse. Hoping they will improve won't make it so, and I was chagrined to see other therapists avoiding their clients' disintegration. None of this fit my fantasy of psychotherapists as heroic salvagers of hurting human souls.

On Powerlessness

There is probably some truth to the saying that a conservative is a liberal who has been mugged. Revising my expectations for what is truly attainable in the therapy office is an ongoing and complex process. I wouldn't be honest if I didn't confess to a somewhat abridged faith in the value of therapy, although I think I am getting better at recognizing which types of situations can benefit from help and which seem to need other, larger community interventions.

Basically, it's all about empowerment. Human (and this includes social and environmental) problems can be stubborn in the face of our efforts to change them. The new activism will focus not on grabbing power in the name of others, but helping those others — whoever they are — to seize it for themselves and do something about their situation. The one thing I wish my supervisors had set me straight on during my training was this: we are powerless in the face of some human problems. It's hard to know how to deal with this powerlessness until you've experienced it yourself. This revelation, in and of itself, will give you a leg up. It makes you push hard in areas where you *do* have power, because the helplessness you have known in others is frightening.

Dealing with Blows to our Idealism

Unfortunately, many concerned people swing to indifference and conservatism after their ideals are dealt a blow. When we are young, we tend to see the world in black and white. As time goes on we begin to see how much the gray area really does matter. Developing a healthy skepticism and revising our ideals doesn't mean giving up all hope for social change. It does mean, however, that you don't avoid the opportunities for maturing that present themselves to you.

If we avoid the passionate excesses of the Sixties, the chance that we will opt for the "Big Chill" option is less likely. Those who cling naively to unreachable ideals often realize later that this inhibited their ability to respond to the world in meaningful ways. After we join the work force, I hope those of us in our twenties will not forget our ideals and will continue to think practically about them. The more of us who can do something socially worthwhile, the more of us who will benefit from the experience and wisdom that come through the process of struggle. We are hardly in a position immediately after college to be very effective in our idealistic efforts. As one activist who runs his own organization said, "I don't like collaborating with academic types or those who just left school. For the most part they talk well, but most of them don't know how to lick a stamp."

It's better to get out in the world for awhile and then reexamine our ideals when we've had enough experience to see how things really work. The activism informed by an "inner workings" knowledge is generally much more effective than the activism of the well-meaning but naive. It is guided by a greater awareness of the legal, educational, and media points of leverage and of resistance in the systems targeted for reform.

Moreover, as time goes on, we become better at listening to what our inner voices have to say as they guide us through the helping process. This can be an incredible resource, and many activists develop — or work primarily from — a deeply felt inner knowledge or sense of mission. Fran Peabody's book *Heart Politics* is a favorite among the interviewees I spoke with on this topic. It is an especially poignant story because of her humble, down-to-earth style and tragic end (she died of AIDS). Soul-making through service is a huge topic that I can only touch on briefly here. If you'd like to explore this area in more depth I also refer you to the writings of Ram Dass (formerly Richard Alpert), especially his lovely book, *How Can I Help?*

Yuppies hardly invented the monster work week. A friend of mine in California who works for an organization called Voter Revolt regularly works sixty-hour weeks. Some days she's sorry she turned down that job she was offered in Paris translating and interpreting for an American company. But when her group wins a tough battle against an unfair insurance company practice, she says the feeling is indescribable, and her offices overflow with riotous celebration.

The activists I interviewed almost overwhelmingly reported that the greatest benefit of working where they do is the quality of the people they work with. They thrive on being surrounded by creative, committed, and caring people trying to make a difference. Such a benefit shouldn't be overlooked. If you really like who you work with, instead of expending energy just tolerating people, you can actually look forward to going in each day — a not inestimable blessing.

How to Live on Less Than $14,000 a Year

OUCH! Economic pain can be harsh. Unfortunately, many of us have to put up with lousy paying jobs at this time in our lives. What to do about it?

You can live quite inexpensively if you're creative about it. The main items in your budget are housing, transportation, food, clothes and entertainment. You probably don't have a whole lot of control over housing. Try to find an acceptable and safe apartment that's toward the low end of rents in your area. Or better yet, move into a group house

---

☐ Ten Good Ways to Save Dough

- ■ Never buy anything in a showroom
- ■ Volunteer for extra shifts at work, even if you don't make much—at least you won't be out spending it
- ■ Don't buy new stuff, but instead try to fix up what you've already got
- ■ Drive old but reliable makes of autos
- ■ Cook and eat at home
- ■ Never fly anywhere
- ■ Avoid expensive hobbies, such as skydiving or sports cars
- ■ Find free fun—dress rehearsals, state parks, public beaches
- ■ Recruit a low-maintenance steady
- ■ Travel light—you might be moving a lot

---

and save on rent that way. Or share a large apartment with a few roommates. There are many other strategies — becoming a house manager or bartering landscape work for rent among them — that can make housing more affordable. Saving money on your housing costs is probably the best way to squeeze big dollars out of your regular monthly outlay. But of course there are an infinite number of ways to economize.

Food Some hints: don't buy processed or ready to eat foods like frozen dinners. The more unprocessed the food, the cheaper and better for you it will be, usually. Stay away from restaurants. You can generally get three meals out of what it costs you to eat out once. Make food instead of buying it already prepared. Making homemade pizza is fun and not all that difficult and much more rewarding than shelling out $15 for a pie delivered to your door. Use meat as one element in a dish you're preparing, rather than as a course in and of itself. Work at your local co-op — you can get a discount that way too. Bring a calculator to the grocery store and comparison shop. Improving your shopping skills can save you a bundle.

Clothes You probably don't need nearly as many as you

☐ Ten Cheap N' Good Foods

- Pasta
- Rice and Beans
- Stir-Fry
- Soups
- Stews
- Chicken
- Burritos and Tacos
- Ramen Noodles
- Couscous
- Salads

might think. Get out of the "new wardrobe for each season" mentality. Sew and repair old sweaters and shirts. Patch your pants or cut them off into shorts. You can find terrific clothes at vintage clothing stores for next to nothing. This can also be fun. Shoes, on the other hand, usually conform to their original owners' feet, so I don't recommend buying used ones. However, knowing a good leather worker or shoe repair shop in town is helpful. Get those loafers resoled and put taps on them if you do a lot of walking.

Entertainment You can find tons of free entertainment out there with just a little research. Music schools offer free recitals, there are inexpensive second-run and repertory movie theaters, free public lectures, art fairs, the list is endless. Check out publications that identify free events in your community. Hanging out with friends is almost always cheap, especially if they are as far off the yuppie track as you are. If your friends live far away, call during the inexpensive hours. You'll get a lot more talk for your buck that way.

Best of all, the wilderness is still free. Spend time in local parks hiking and biking. Take a picnic and a hacky sack. Go out to a local wetlands park an hour before sunrise and climb a tree. You'll hear the frost breaking off every leaf and twig and a rising crescendo of bird songs. Some of my friends claim there is no better way to start the day. Camping is cheap once you acquire or borrow the basic gear, and the solace and beauty afforded by our nation's lakes and mountains is stunning.

Transportation Try using public transportation when you can. Cars are the primary source of pollution in America and are often unnecessary. It costs an average of $5,000 a year to keep a car in service including insurance, incidental repairs and upkeep, parking, gas, fines, stickers, et cetera. Public transportation costs a fraction of that. Or get a used mountain bike, a solid lock, and some bus tokens for rainy days. Borrow a friend's car for the afternoon you have an interview or need to run errands in exchange for filling the tank with gas.

Most importantly, it helps if you can think of this process as a game or a challenge. If you start feeling bogged down and deprived, it can bum you out. Sometimes you just have to break down and splurge. A nutritionist friend who raised three kids on a meager salary recommends the occasional indulgence: "If you start feeling deprived, it can hurt. Once in awhile you just have to cut loose and do something just for you. Go out to dinner, or buy a shiny new bauble for yourself." As a generation we should prepare to live more economically, and more responsibly—it's easier on both the world's environmental resources and our own personal resources.

Creature Comforts and Consumption

We should at all times resist the temptation to give primacy to the material addictions our culture supports. Creature comforts and easy credit are waiting to seduce you at every turn. We all have times when we flip through a magazine, see a full-page ad for a jet ski with a built-in CD player and portable bar and say, "Hey, I *need* that!" Just learn to wait ten minutes, laugh at yourself, and then reassess whether or not you really do need it.

We all consume; it's just a matter of how much of our consumption is planned and considered. Can you spend an afternoon downtown without blowing any money on impulse buys? Have you priced a product or service that catches your eye elsewhere? Do you really need it now? Can you fix what you already have rather than replace it?

Buy used. It's a worthwhile form of recycling obsolescent products of our too disposability-oriented society. Let your friends know if you're looking for a sofa, a bike, or a hammock, maybe they can turn one up for you. Garage sales are fun ways to meet people and a good source of kitchenware and furniture. Check out your local second-hand stores, like Goodwill Industries and Salvation Army. These are often sponsored by local hospitals or churches. And of course, there is a real art to buying a good used car. Have it looked at by a mechanic or a friend who knows a thing or two about compression. Don't forget that new cars lose 10 to 20 percent of their value the minute your drive them off the dealer's lot.

The Credit Crunch

There's no better time to get your first credit card than when you graduate from college, if you haven't already gotten one. Creditors know that in demographic terms college graduates are good credit risks, so they'll often bombard new grads with opportunities to open Visa, MasterCard, department store, gasoline, and even jewelry store credit lines. Take advantage of this opportunity — a few years down the road and you won't be quite so fresh and appealing in statistical terms (making your measly salary and struggling with your new and burdensome financial obligations), and you might find it harder to break into the great American credit runaround. Like it or not, a good credit rating is important in our society, and you should do what you can to protect yours.

Many twentysomethings get into credit trouble during their first few years in the working world, for a couple of different reasons. Some are just inexperienced and lacking in discipline regarding the management of their finances; soon their outflow is exceeding their income, and before long they find themselves toting a four-figure debt load. Others genuinely need to use their credit to keep their heads above water, especially if confronted with some sort of emergency situation that requires a dramatic and immediate outlay of cash.

You can hope that your presently paltry salary will soon grow enough to allow you to pay off these debts, but you're best off doing everything you can to prevent carrying any sort of balance on any sort of credit card. Those of us paying off students loans or financing car purchases already have it hard enough. But even for those of us without any other debts, credit card costs are pernicious, and death on any ambitions we might have to save money. Why? Interest rates pushing 20 percent, for starters. Big banks across America are desperately trying to pay for their Eighties excesses. Some are staying afloat solely by way of the profits they're raking in with the obscene rates they're charging for credit cards.

Don't do it. Bite the bullet. Allowing yourself to go into the credit card hole will reduce the freedom and flexibility that are the best part of life in your twenties. What's more, it will indicate to your elders that you're not yet as responsible as you want them to believe you to be. But most of all, it's just plain foolish. The cost of credit in the Nineties is preposterous. Don't become a slave to your plastic.

Wealth and Isolation

As you make more money in America you can buy more comfort, convenience, and mobility. Unfortunately (or fortunately, depending on your perspective), you also become more isolated; your house or apartment is farther from the neighbors, you now have to drive everywhere, and nobody comes by to borrow a wrench or a cup of sugar. Many of the people in their twenties whom I interviewed did not include extreme isolation as one of their troubles, probably because they often didn't have much money. Interacting with others allows a glimmer of a community to start up as you meet people during dog walks, over an open car hood, or when you're allergic to their incense.

"Success prudes," like their counterparts in the sexual realm, don't tend to make a lot of friends because they over-work themselves and have little or no time to put into a friendship, often associate only with the people they work with, and tend to be less accepting of other people's differences.

A woman serving me drinks one night recounted how she left a high-powered job in Washington to become a waitress. Belonging to a community became very important to her and she deliberately sought out restaurants that had a repu-tation as being places where there was a positive sense of community. She felt the lack of community so acutely in D.C. that she decided to change her entire orientation to life.

In short, living on less is not living less good. Candlelight, human warmth, free recreation, and chipping in together with friends for fun and adventure all remain viable and in-expensive means of enjoying life. Many swear by living in the minimalist mode. More older people than you would think look back at their impoverished early years as the richest and most exciting of their lives — they learned then what was important and what wasn't.

SEVEN

Relationships Versus Manipulationships

WHY are relationships such a big deal in our twenties? For the same reasons they are a big deal at every other stage of life: romanticized notions of love, the desire for sex and attention, peer pressure, social status, and adventure. But bonding at this stage of life is complicated by our generation's transience, uncertainty about what we want, and relative lack of experience.

No treatment of these issues would be complete without recognizing that falling in love is hardly a rational process. A noted family therapist by the name of Jay Haley once said "We're all dealing with relationships. We're either in one, getting out of one, looking for one, or running like hell." One's twenties are incomplete if we haven't fallen for someone, somewhere along the line. At any rate, we cannot choose the experience itself, but we can choose how to respond to the experience. When falling in love, it's easy not to think too much about how healthy we or our prospective partner is. But this is exactly what we need to focus on if we want relationships that will be satisfying and rewarding. So, now's the time to sharpen your first-meeting, lightning-quick, mental-calculation skills regarding a person's desirability, sanity, or desperation. Be careful to avoid stereotyping. In this matter, irreverence will serve you better than cynicism.

The Basics

It might be useful to cover briefly what is already well known and documented in the psychological research about how we pair up. Generally speaking, we "hit it off" with people from similar socioeconomic and racial backgrounds. We would do well not to underestimate the role of class in how and why we choose certain people. This is important in ways we tend to ignore, submerged in our consciousness. We tend to like people of similar intelligence, with similar social values, who enjoy a similar perspective on life. We also tend to have at least some common interests, but of course having a balance of similar and different interests can be stimulating as well.

Excitement, stimulation, and frolickability are the staples of an enjoyable and nourishing jaunt in love's garden. But strength and stability are the staples of any such venture that lasts more than three weeks. If you can provide these on a consistent basis, people who share your particular chemistry will most likely be attracted to you and stick like glue. You're in especially good shape if the seven-year-olds in you get along well. Falling in love can be one of the most exhilarating experiences we are likely to have in our lifetimes. But it is also perhaps the one most fraught with thorny patches.

Everyone needs to know how to stand on their own. In other words, you don't want two people leaning on each other, each moaning and blaming the other for not propping them up. It is much better if two people stand up, look one another right in the eye, and gracefully forge as equal a bond as they dare. How capable are you of standing on your own? How capable are you of doing your part to hammer out a mutually agreed-upon solution to a thorny relationship conflict?

One other important area is public comfort: basically,

how at ease we are in our partner's company. This includes how affectionate we like to be in public, and what each considers appropriate dress and social behavior. One of my interviewees reported that one of the things he likes best about his partner is that she never embarrasses him. If she doesn't know much about a topic when in a discussion at a party, she keeps to herself; when she knows a little, she covers herself well; and when in her area of expertise she seldom condescends or lets irresponsible statements slip by. In his social circles, this is an important quality. Nobody likes to be seen with somebody who talks about a lot of inconsequential baloney or makes a lot of ridiculous pronouncements. One friend reports that one of his dates talked about her haircut for fifty-six nonstop minutes (he timed it in disbelief).

And of course, there are the sparks of physical attraction. Although this can be easily under or overrated, it is important and we would do well to value it appropriately. Be wary of how well you "match" with another's sexual preferences. A friend just concluded a long and painful relationship with a man who finally was able to admit to himself that he is gay. Thank god they weren't married first — this would have really been trouble. Another person I interviewed went out with a woman a few times, and one night she told him that she was bisexual. Being an open-minded sort, this was not too shocking to him, but he did say, "Look, that doesn't sound too great to me. If we do go out, not only do I have to worry about all the other guys walking around, I have to worry about all of the women, too."

The Good, The Bad, and The Ugly

The good things in life are rarely free of fear. Part of learning about these good things is facing the fear that surrounds them, and few things can seem more fearsome than the quest for love. Now, being loved feels pretty fabulous all over. If we cast ourselves with any sincerity at all into this arena of risk and discovery, of intimacy and sweetness, of knowledge and vulnerability, we can't help but be transformed. If we can get through the fear to reach a state of true intimacy with our beloved, we can learn more about what really matters to us, get nearer to our creative selves, experience new and wonderful feelings, and get glimpses, however fleeting, of vibrant meaning in our lives. And besides, with a supportive partner, you can put off laughing too loudly at your own jokes for whole afternoons at a time. Companionship is fine, but intimacy is raw delight.

Unfortunately, there are a lot of people around who have grown up assuming that if you want to get anything in this world, you have to play games and be manipulative. Fortunately, people who are good at being able to say what they want are generally good at getting it. If they are fair about it, they may even see the value of helping someone they care about get what they want in return. So, get good at being direct about what you want and need. Everyone in your life will appreciate it and you won't have to put up with as much social static.

But beyond some mild community pressure, there are no relationship police. There is no one out there to enforce fidelity, promises, and fairness. This is why we need to seek ways to make relationships more fair. In order to understand more fully the distinctions I'm trying to draw here, let's consider some definitions. A relationship is a bond between two people based on respect, equality, consideration, mutual affection, and honesty. Some of the things common to good relationships are: an emphasis on being together, not on getting something from the other person; having fun together; some ability to negotiate and resolve the conflicts that inevitably crop up; and some reciprocal exchange when it comes to emotional support.

A manipulationship, on the other hand is characterized by the shrewd, self-interested use of emotional influence, particularly in an unfair way. Some of the characteristics common to manipulationships are: underhanded, indirect communications — hitting below the belt during fights, temper tantrums, suicide threats, or other behavior directed toward one person getting their way no matter what; overemphasis on sex instead of love; one person essentially footing the bill for much of what the couple does together; false promises, a pattern of unreliable behavior, lies, infidelities, secrets kept about infidelities, et cetera; and discomfort with the hows and whens and how oftens of the sexual relationship.

It should be noted that many relationships are perceived as manipulationships only after the fact ("I can't believe I slept with that. . . "). But there are real differences that can be ascertained at the time, and these can help you make a judgment about whether it's healthy to stay in it.

It seems to me that women are particularly susceptible to being manipulated because of all the romanticizations crammed into their heads, from their Barbie years straight through college. It's helpful sometimes to disregard how someone says they feel about you and ask yourself how their actual behavior effects you. Just because someone says they love you doesn't mean that you are loved. Only you can answer that question. We've all heard people try to rationalize piss-poor treatment (hitting, verbal abuse, mental cruelty) by saying, "but he says he loves me so I guess that makes it O.K." A better question might be, "despite what he says his feelings are for me, do I feel loved by him?"

There is one quality that will distinguish a relationship from a manipulationship 95 percent of the time: vulnerability. When people become close, they naturally reveal aspects of themselves to the other that are hard to talk about, especially experiences of weakness, hurt, pain, and fear. Why is this so difficult? Because this is the person that you most want to impress with your strength and brilliance so that you will appear attractive. Kind of ironic, eh? But the strength that couples derive from their willingness to be vulnerable with each other is a major foundation of love. True vulnerability is generally not present in manipulationships because you don't want someone you're trying to use to have anything over you.

Priorities

By now, most of you have probably had some sort of relationship with at least a couple of people who were in some kind of unhealthy condition. These situations test your personal boundaries. Should you try to help? How? How much? What if they don't seem to be getting better? How much is too much? What then?

Some of you may not have much confidence in your own emotional health. I know I often don't feel brimming over with confidence in this area. If you feel similarly, don't worry. A person who wants to be aware of these issues and strives actively to overcome their problems is always healthier than one who isn't, or just doesn't care.

I encourage you to think more critically about emotional health, both your own and that of the people you choose to surround yourself with. And I mean more than what we usually think of as relationship health here. I mean, asking ourselves questions such as, "how kind is their soul?" and reaching deep into ourselves to see how much we trust them.

A country singer once said, "I've been rich and I've been poor. Rich is better." The same goes for relationships and manipulationships. The latter have the uncanny ability to burn you up for years afterwards. One must distinguish, however, between people who are a bit crazier than the rest of us, and those who are sane but manipulative. Sometimes it's not that the crazy ones don't mean well; they're just a little screwed-up and under different circumstances would never act so poorly. Once they get it together they can be real sweethearts. These types are actually a safer bet than the

113

out-and-out manipulators because they are not out to
squeeze you for everything you're worth. Of course, the
worst-case scenario is coming upon someone both crazy *and*
manipulative. Far too many people suffered the shock of
recognition when viewing films like *Dangerous Liaisons* and
Fatal Attraction.

Subvertising

Advertising is one source of our confusion about relationships. We are inundated by hundreds of images of pretty
people every day. In our culture, good looks have come to
be associated with health and the good life. In point of fact,
they have very little to do with how good a person someone
is. This is not to discount the exciting reactions we all can
have to physically beautiful people, but is merely to point
out that it can be a little like raiding an empty refrigerator.

Most commercials are set in perfect worlds where all your
problems can be solved, if you only purchase Brand X. Such
fantasies, harmless as they may seem, mislead. They set us
up to start believing in those picture-perfect worlds for ourselves, and for the feelings of inadequacy that inevitably
come with not having the right wardrobe, lip gloss, or
whatever.

We swim in a sea of ads that all try to sell us new cars,
clothes, looks, and smells with sex appeal. Even Mr. Good-
wrench is getting in on the act. Every day our consciousness
is more disastrously overpopulated by these advertisements
and their messages. The result: the usual consequences of
congestion — confusion, pollution, numbness, and the need
to reduce the population.

Living in a culture saturated with promotional messages
warps our perception of value. One basically stable woman
I know of moved here from Lebanon and within about six
months had developed an eating disorder, bulimia. In retro-

spect, she feels that it was brought on by all the pressure she experienced here to be thin. Advertising is all about glamor and envy. It does not give us any information about real life, just fantasy.

We cannot help but be influenced by advertising. Not many of us want fat partners and this is due in part to the anorexic standards models and movie stars and other supposedly "ideal" women are held to. The point is this: we need to focus more on what's really important in order to correct this bias in our culture.

In order to get real we need to leave behind commercial fantasies of "the good life," the "perfect partner," and the "right image," for ourselves. Experiencing meaning in relationships is very different from feeling bolstered by brand names and shopping sprees. There are multiple levels on which we need to think about life and health: individual, familial, communal, societal. The rest is just flash.

Unfortunately, when confronted with pseudo-values — rich men, pretty women — people tend to discard common sense. They too easily forget what underlies a healthy and rewarding bond. The allure that powerful men exert over women is legendary, but so is their greater susceptibility to destructive and unhealthy tendencies. For men, tales of destruction at the hands of beautiful women are legion. Only after getting over bad relationships and tracing their scars do some people learn how to articulate their own vision of what bonding with another person is really about. Often times this involves bucking the cultural lies that surround these values.

Ungodly Expectations

It is all too easy to slip into placing too much emphasis on romance. This can become ugly when something traumatic happens and it feels like a rug is yanked out from underneath you, only to reveal a cracked floor that's not as strong as you remembered. So concentrate on building a solid floor, for there are no guarantees that even people you trust and cherish will stick around as long as you want.

The romantic myths of our culture have created unreachable expectations and place unbearable strains on bonds. They are so seductive we somehow assume that almost any problem can be solved by "falling in love" and "settling down." Our culture conveys the notion that marriage works by magic if it is between the "right" people, and if it doesn't work that means it was between the "wrong" people. This is the formula Hollywood romance and implies a predetermined arrangement "meant" or usually "not meant" to be that involves little work or compromise.

All of this might be quite funny if it wasn't so widely believed and so devastating in its effects. When marriages fail, people blame it on the nature of marriage, or the "opposite" sex, the specific partner, the stars, the time in life when they married, the chemistry, or falling out of love. Few of us are prepared for the simple but completely engulfing state of marriage, or even think we need to be. The romantic myth is all we're given to go on. Instead, try thinking of marriage as exchanging the set of single problems — loneliness, boredom — for the set of couple problems — cooperation, trust, fidelity.

Three guys in a post-doctoral program felt they had it all: looks, charm, and credentials they weren't shy about showing off at a bar they typically haunted "trolling for babes," as they say. A couple of their friends weren't so sanguine about their futures, though. "They think they're the ideal," one said, "macho and successful and all that, but really these guys are going to create a lot of misery for themselves and their families. Sure they'll attract some babe and have a family, but they're not at all interested in relationships or communication or anything. It's so ironic that in many ways, they are the ideal our culture upholds, but when it comes to being real, they're just emotional adolescents."

116

Some Cautionary Tales

I once fell, with frightening results, for a gorgeous woman who turned out to be self-consumed and (from my perspective at least) perhaps even a little psycho. I would get hysterical calls in the middle of the night during which she would threaten to hurt herself if I didn't come right over. Then there would be long periods where she would pretend that nothing was wrong. Sure, anyone can act a little unsettled from time to time, but there was a sharp and sinister edge to the way she was handling things that should have clued me in. She saw other men behind my back, and one old boyfriend in particular kept fading in and out of the picture. Of course, this all happened when I was young and stupid, a long long time ago.

Eventually it just wore me out, and I broke the relationship off. Some time passed, and I noticed that a few of my friends were acting strangely around me. Some digging on my part uncovered the fact that she had gone to several people within our close-knit community and asserted that I had done something truly horrible to her (I still don't know the specifics). Several of my friends stopped talking to me altogether and to this day have never approached me to find out my version of the story. Just retelling this anecdote stings. Manipulationships have a psychic, social, and emotional price tag too steep to bear for long.

Few say it better than Dr. Sonya Friedman (*Men Are Just Desserts, Smart Cookies Don't Crumble*), a well-known Detroit-area psychologist. She writes, "Some of us make a huge investment in a relationship when it begins. We have no real sense of who the person is. We only know who we hope he or she is. Then the reality sets in. The man who said, 'You pick the restaurant and make the reservations' and made your choices appear wonderful is now seen as not willing to take the time to do these things himself. The woman

117

who wouldn't be seen without her makeup on because she always wanted to look her best for you is now viewed as narcissistic and nonexistent beyond her appearance."

Interpersonal health is not a topic that is very well understood in our culture. Where do we learn about relationships? In school? On TV? At church? In sports-related activities? Most of us would probably say at home, a notoriously intermittent source of good information.

Our culture is unforthcoming about the need to develop relationship skills such as conflict resolution, negotiation, respectful confrontation, sensitivity, and power-sharing (although by our twenties most of us have learned the importance of communication). This is a crucial area of our lives that is left up to accident, luck, and unspoken cultural entitlements (i.e., men control the money, women rear the children). Somehow couples are just supposed to "make it happen." But sometimes relationships take a lot of work. Lots of therapists are in business because people lack these rudimentary relationship skills.

A teacher of English as a Second Language was drawn into a relationship with an older man by his charm and intelligence, his big house, the fact that he was already well established professionally, and by the fact that she hoped the relationship would offer her the security she wanted to start a family. In short, he represented a near-ideal "success object." There were some serious downsides to the relationship—their age discrepancy (15 years), his children from a previous marriage, and some cultural differences—specifically, his general attitude toward women. For whatever reason, she ignored these issues. One night they were out listening to a band at a nightclub and one of the musicians made a lewd gesture toward her with his horn. Her boyfriend just laughed and went along with it.

Of all her friends, only one told her how afraid she was for her, even crying in her presence over how sad and worried she was about what she saw as a daily accumulation of small degradations. Later, after several months of ups and downs, this teacher finally realized that her boyfriend would never want to have kids and her unhappiness reached a breaking point. Finally, she was able to extricate herself.

Eventually she asked her other friends about why they didn't try to point out more of the downsides of the relationship to her. They said they felt that it wasn't their business or that they figured there must be some good things about the relationship they couldn't see. Fair enough. But she has since grown very close with the friend who did warn her. And now, whenever she starts a new relationship, her mother asks her what that friend thinks of the new guy!

Another interviewee married a dashing older man straight out of high school. He apparently had inherited an investment portfolio and was well connected in the community. This relationship was her dream come true, until she discovered that he would leave her and their two children at odd hours of the night and started taking a lot of mysterious phone calls. She feared that he had a mistress. As it turned out, the situation was far more alarming. After the relationship soured and turned abusive, it turned out he was a major cocaine kingpin. He was at such pains to have a "respectable" family that he expended huge amounts of energy maintaining this secret by constantly moving the family and leaving behind a trail of lies and deceit.

Emotional Celibacy

Consider taking time out to be celibate. And I don't necessarily mean just sexually celibate, but emotionally celibate as well. It's easy to get caught up in the dating scene: who's dating whom, who's waiting in the wings, what'll happen if Rick breaks up with Carolyn, and so on. This consumes energy in the form of hopes, fantasies, phone calls, unreturned phone calls, endless gossip, and calculation of chances. Drop out of circulation for awhile. Don't be asocial, just stop hunting. "After my last girlfriend and I broke up I realized that I had been involved with someone for the last eight years of my life," a young musician recounted. "It's time for a break."

I'm going to try and sell you on singledom for a little bit here. When else do you have such command over your time and money? When else are you free from the subtle pressures to be positive or sensitive when you don't particularly feel like it? And best of all, in addition to relief from a million little annoyances — from what they do to your Sunday newspaper to how you treat their more dubious friends — you never, never have to break up.

One friend reached his breaking point after several years of almost constantly being attached to someone. He started dating again and soon found someone to whom he felt drawn. "I think we both liked each other, but we were both too shy to do anything about it. But I'm the guy, so that means it was up to me to make the first move, right? *Not.*" He rebelled against the pressure and decided to chill by himself for awhile.

We are too young to be fully aware of our emotional and sexual dependencies on others. Now is the time to learn to take care of ourselves. This doesn't necessarily mean that we have to become rugged individualists struggling for autonomy at any cost. It means we have to try to develop a social support network that doesn't rely solely on a few people, or worst of all, one person. Learning to meet our own needs puts us in an excellent position if and when we get involved with someone later in life.

Focus on the question, "Where am I going?" instead of whether or not anyone is going along with you at this point. This is perhaps *the* question we need to answer in our twenties. Only after we have some good clues about where we ourselves are headed are we ready to find out who it is we want joining us along our life's course. The order here is crucial. If you bind your fate to someone else's before you have a good sense of what you yourself are about, you are asking too much of that relationship.

A Time to Stay and a Time to Stay Away

If you've been feeling off-center, it's O.K. to stay away from relationships until you feel more confident that you wouldn't be hurting people. Inflicting an unbalanced self on others is hardly fair, especially if you might trespass important personal or sexual boundaries (knowing which aspects of yourself not to trust is helpful). Be a little careful of anyone "on the rebound." This is a tough call, because certain people don't become available very often, and maybe you've been waiting for an opening to make your move. The time taken to get to know someone well is rarely wasted. If people are smart enough to respect both you and their own needs, they'll wait before rushing in.

The majority of us who could be moderately good for someone (or at least not intentionally pernicious) might consider activities other than "dating." One friend says that he always asks someone to join him in an activity that he would enjoy doing on his own, like taking a walk. As long as it provides time and space to get acquainted, you can then be free of the pressure of a "date." Dating prescribes that a relationship, if it is to continue, be "romantic." Unless the attraction is immediate and irresistible, at this stage few people know enough to decide that. Much of getting a relationship off to a good start involves information exchange. You need to feel reasonably sure this person is someone you trust, and someone whose company you really enjoy, before you proceed. If you "date" first, then all you'll know is "not romance" instead of "possible friend," and the latter could in the end be quite a bit more important. The possible friendship starts from a deficit perspective.

If your "friend" isn't capable of having friendships with members of the opposite sex, this doesn't bode well for their character: consider letting the relationship go. Each person has their own criteria for what an acceptable relationship is, so stick to yours. If you've been getting some funny feelings about this person and you're not sure if things are going well, check it out. Chances are you're probably right — they probably aren't. Write in your journal or talk to a friend. Then, when you feel like you understand the issues a bit better, set your partner down and lay it all out for them.

There is definitely a time and place for breaking things off. If things just aren't working out according to your own criteria, and you don't have a lot of ideas for overhauling trouble spots (or it seems like too much work), it's probably a good time to end it. We've all known people who have stayed in destructive relationships for too long. When things are over, let them be over. Have the courage to split and move on.

Feeling a Little Too Single?

Loneliness, of course, can be tough too. I'm not a big adherent of the shopping bag approach to meeting people. If singles ads work for you, great. There are so many different levels at which relationships have to mesh that I'm always surprised when this works for friends. But if you want to meet even more new people, get out there. Be persistently social. Persistence is just as important in meeting people as it is in job hunting. Take up contra dancing. Go to church. Join a cycling association and get in shape. It's not always easy to be brave, but put people who like each other in the same room and they'll figure out some way to exchange come-hither glances and witty repartee. Flirt away. What have you got to lose? For an excellent and humorous treatment of this subject, see Cynthia Heimel's chapter on flirting in her book *Sex Tips for Girls*.

Of course, there's a lot of warped stuff going on out there in the singles world. What do you expect in a country where people make and sell their own home porno movies? And if there wasn't that to deal with, even dating seemingly stable and sane people can be stressful. All of the "am I attractive? where do I stand? will we get along?" kinds of stuff can be exhausting until you can achieve real intimacy with someone. This, of course, is assuming you get along well enough to *want* to be that intimate.

There are three primary reasons why we don't meet more potential partners than we do: anxiety about rejection, fear of rejection, and, most importantly, complete and utter terror of rejection. So, don't be rejecting. If someone seems interested in you but doesn't really pique your interest, be nice about it. It could be you the next time.

Insofar as rejection hurts (and it certainly does), we fear it. However, as time goes on, you realize that it's O.K. that not everyone is going to like you. This makes it easier to take risks. Then, as your confidence and sense of timing grow, your comfort with yourself will make you easier to like.

When you meet someone new, notice if you find yourself relishing their eyes. If you detect the practiced look of a hardened flirt, proceed with caution. Try to keep the mixed messages to a minimum as well. Don't flirt heavily with people unless you are at least mildly interested in them. And a little bit of etiquette: results are results, people. If you've been pursuing someone and they haven't returned your last two or three calls, drop it. Don't harass someone.

Try to avoid the "fifteen-second crowd." In an effort to display a chic cynicism, these people say, "You know, it's getting to the point where when I meet someone, I can tell in the first fifteen seconds whether we might be compatible." This is an almost laughable self-delusion. Many people report that they were hardly thunderstruck when they first met their eventual spouse.

This is also a time when some people begin to experiment with dating a greater variety of people than before. Others tend to become pickier (and lonelier on weekends). Consider taking advantage of the opportunities to date people whom you might not consider at first to be your "type." Many people report that they have never been able to sustain a working relationship with someone who fits their type in their whole life. You can stretch yourself by hanging out with people not quite on your familiar wavelength. Besides, how would you feel if you overheard someone say at a party that you were cute, but "not really my type." They don't even know you! You would resent being stereotyped.

Sex: Some Mostly Good News

Ah, sex. So much to talk about, so little space. Sex is fun! Sex is complicated! Sex is profound! For most, sexuality is an intensely private and sacred realm. It can be one of the most grandly sensual, replenishing, and beautiful experiences in life. But at the same time sex is frightening because it can make us feel so vulnerable.

The most important suggestion about sexuality that can be made (one particularly defensible in this era) is to encourage you to reserve sex for people you love. The second most important suggestion is to encourage you to communicate about your sexual feelings, likes, and dislikes, directly and during sex. This is much more important than dieting or quitting smoking when it comes to pleasing partners. Sure it might seem a little unromantic or awkward to say "move a little over there" during the heat of the moment. But if it's heat you want, some well-timed words are a sure way to stoke the fire.

Generally speaking, having an excellent physical connection, nice as it can be, is not always a sound basis for being in a relationship. Real love should be self-enlarging and you limit yourself by merely taking a recreational approach to sexuality. However, don't underestimate the importance of a strong sexual attraction. It is very important, especially considering the commitment required to overcome some of the temptations you will inevitably face if you make a long-term monogamous commitment.

There is an important transition a couple makes after the first few times they make love. After the taut springs of desire are uncoiled, the "litmus rest" immediately afterwards begins when you think to yourself, "do I really want to be here now?" Do you still feel warm and comfortable? Are you telling jokes, or are you running off to the shower, refrigerator, or worse yet, heading home? Sad to say, but men often fall in love with people after they are attracted to them. Women often become more attracted to men after they fall in love. I will indulge no more gross stereotypes here, but I've seen it too often to let this pattern slip by unremarked.

Much more could be said about talking back to the inhumane voices of your sexual conditioning, and about gender expectations. Some of the descriptions of lovemaking in popular novels are almost hilariously ludicrous. Men with "white hot swords", and so on. Men are often made to feel that their ability to "perform" is the most important thing about their sexuality. This can be a real hindrance to sexual intimacy. Conversely, women are often made to feel that they should place their partner's pleasure above their own. These and other stupid messages keep many people from sexual enjoyment. Certainly more could be said about how frustrating sexual hang-ups and problems can be. But, whatever the issues or "problems" may be, be careful with the love you feel. The power of sexuality to connect you to another human being is just this side of a miracle. The eroticism of sex with love has the potential to cut to the core of your being. Safeguard its ability to transform you.

Sex: Some Mostly Bad News

Unfortunately, for many people sex is not a particularly cheery topic. Studies show that about one third of adult women have had their soft tissues, bones, and spirits violated by rape or attempted rape. Most of them reported that the assaults were by people they knew, and many of them were by people with whom they had had sex with previously. This is a huge problem that is reinforced at many different levels of our society and I wouldn't want to be glib in offering up facile solutions.

For men, however, no means no. You do more damage than you might think if you push sex on others. Just because you have an erection doesn't mean your companion at the moment is obliged to do something about it. Just to be sure to maintain honest contact with his partner, one friend told me that he always asks, the moment before they merge, if his partner is sure she wants to do this. Even with lovers he has been with for months and years. This is a solid and conscientious suggestion that your partners will appreciate.

Know that if you place your pleasure and need for power so far above another's well-being, that you are hurting someone else and withering your own soul. Do everything in your power to be a trustworthy person. It's a complicated issue, but before we can get around to addressing the inequities of power in society and how to change them, let's do what we can to prevent horrifying events like rape, sexual assault, and harassment. Challenge male friends who brag about this sort of bullshit (definitely easier said than done, although you might be surprised by the respect you get from some quarters). If you're not sure about your own behavior, talk it over with some sensitive friends. If you have a lot more questions, see if there are any sexual assault prevention centers connected to your local college or community agency. These organizations offer many educational and counseling services and are just beginning to get the national exposure they need. "Strange as it may sound, I find it heartening that some guys come into my office and want to talk about whether they raped or pushed sex on someone the night before," a student counselor relates. "There just wasn't that level of awareness before. I like to think we can continue to educate people about these issues and channel some of the controversy into growth and changed behavior for a lot of others."

The mean age of sexual perpetrators is going down, and studies show that the more pornography one is exposed to, the more violent it has to become for one to be aroused. This is all very scary stuff; we are just beginning to address how sexual exploitation affects power relationships, history, and gender inequality.

Making It Work

I believe there are three main issues in most relationships: power, intimacy, and commitment. You can assess any and every bond along these lines and get a pretty good sense of how balanced the relationship is. For instance, a graduate student in English literature described a relationship (living together) in which both intimacy and commitment were strong, but where his partner would often unilaterally make big financial decisions. She clearly grabbed more power, causing a lot of tension.

A chemist relished the sparkling intimacy and balanced decision-making of a new romance, but when it came to commitment, she found her normally talkative partner full of strange silences and lots of transparent "let's-just-live-in-the-moment" reassurances. After a lot of back and forth and a painful separation, she later found out it took her promising prospect three years just to get a magazine subscription.

Obviously, these issues are linked; commitment and intimacy overlap to some degree, and the person who has the least commitment to a relationship usually has the most power. Despite this fact, many people prefer to feel like they are the one who is most in love because of the soul-throttling nature of the experience: see the poems of W.H. Auden.

Couples usually come to recognize which partner has the most investment in the relationship fairly early on. It becomes apparent that the one with the least commitment has more power because they set the tone of the relationship, decide how much time you will spend together, and when you can stay over. This can be very frustrating, particularly because they will be setting things up to suit themselves (at a lower level of commitment) and not you, and you won't be getting what you want.

A couple who met while walking their dogs began to date after flirting by the lake all afternoon. He wanted to continue to see other people, and as time went on she felt increasingly hurt by this. Eventually, she sat him down and told him what she wanted and needed: more. He agreed to be her steady boyfriend but admitted he was a little afraid of commitment. Seeing as how they were friends, though, he wasn't afraid of her. They're doing quite well now, thanks to her directness and sensitivity to her own needs and feelings. This was an instructive story for me, in that it is easy to confuse fear of commitment with fear of an individual. I suppose it's more polite to say to someone that you are merely afraid of commitment if you're resisting getting involved with them. But it's interesting to note for yourself that there is something you're not quite comfortable with about that person.

Over time, the forms that power in relationships take and the tenor of intimacy can change. Many women become high-power people in their careers, and this scares many of their husbands, who fear the "Mr. Marie Osmond" syndrome. At a party, they will be approached, recognized, and introduced as the spouse of a respected professional in the community; thus, instead of being known as "Mr. Joe Osmond" or whatever, one is instead known as "Mr. Marie Osmond."

When it comes to power, my advice is to try to balance it out. Switch off when planning activities and making decisions. You plan the first half of the evening and let them plan the second. Bend a little, and see if they bend in return. This is a good indicator of how much someone values the give-and-take that relationships need. If people are mature enough to overcome their initial desire to do what they want first in the interest of what's best for the relationship, they're better-suited to forging a stronger union. Delaying temporary gratification for fuller, more long-term satisfaction is crucial to both individual and relationship survival.

No couple is ever perfectly equal or completely satisfied in all three areas. But sharing and compromise are essential to any relationship. It can feel like work sometimes. A happily married social worker admits "I can't believe the amount of shit I have to put up with," but in the next breath maintains that it's worth it.

What You're Looking For

During our early twenties, most of us are in an "experimental" mode when it comes to dating and relationships. However, at some point, often after we've been out of school for a few years, we begin to enter the "agenda" mode. This is when we begin to look for something more definite, and for a more definite commitment. As one interviewee described it, "At this point in my life, I'm a vegetarian. Although I'm not judgmental of people who aren't vegetarians, I just don't see how I'll be able to wake up in the morning with my partner, run to the fridge so we can make breakfast, and see big chunks of animal flesh oozing blood onto the bottom shelf. And that's just a small example. I guess I'm becoming choosier when it comes to people. I want someone without a lot of past entanglements and issues to work through."

She spoke about how she feels both her life and her goals were taking on more definition, and that this meant that she really didn't want to experiment much more. The problem I often see with twentysomething relationships is that two people are in these two different modes and don't respect the appropriateness of that mode for the other person. In other words, you've got one partner pushing for commitment, and the other pushing for open-endedness. They both think the other is "wrong," when in all fairness each person makes this transition in their own way and at their own pace. Unfortunately, there's no easy way out of this standoff. Nobody has to make a commitment they don't want to make. As time goes on, people usually become either more ready to make a long-term commitment or more certain they won't.

When it comes to commitment, only the caterpillar knows when it's ready to become a butterfly. Cocoons generally don't respond to speeches urging them to become butterflies before they're ready, however impassioned the tone. Believe that people know themselves and know what's best for them. They usually do.

Communication

Communication problems run the range from simple verbal misunderstandings to out-and-out hatred. Sometimes, through false assumptions and judgments, we become experts at misreading each other. Men and women have different communication styles and it can be helpful to explore these varying assumptions and patterns. For more on this topic see the best-seller, *You Just Don't Understand: Women and Men in Conversation*, by Deborah Tannen.

When communicating, caution is required in specifying individual interpretations of certain key phrases. Ask lots of questions like, "What does that mean to you?" or "When you say you love me does that start down there and move up here, or start up here and move down there, or start down there and stay down there?" Be watchful of your individual understandings of big-and-bumpies like "monogamy," "business trip," and "*one* bite of ice cream." The point is, make sure you have common definitions so that you proceed with the ground rules understood by all parties.

Homo Conflictus

Couples face a major hurdle about a year or so into a relationship. They want to stay in love, yet they have to find a way of letting the other know what really bugs them. In short, you have to start to deal with unpleasantness. Lots of relationships and marriages founder because they can't seem to get beyond this stage.

Basically, what we need to get straight with our partners at this stage is how they want us to communicate feedback/bad news to them. For any long-term relationship, it's safe to assume that the need for real discussion is going to be there. For instance, someone might say, "I need you to tell me these things as nicely as possible, with lots of support, because I get upset if I feel like you are criticizing my character." Or someone might say, "I need you to be direct because when I feel guilt-tripped I shut down to you." Another useful way of communicating gripes to each other is to make positive "It's important to me that . . . " sorts of statements. For instance, someone might say, "It's important to me that you pay this bill by Friday." That way, the person knows that if they don't do it, they have not expressed respect for their partner's priorities and feelings. Better yet, they can avoid corrosive nagging and pestering. It's a very simple and mature way to cope with situations that often get mired in guilt, accusation, and counter-accusation.

If we get things like this straight, then there are some good ground rules set up that help us to manage conflict and make it less explosive and destructive. And this is very important to the success of a long-term relationship. Why? Because if we give our partner feedback in the way they've requested and they still don't make some changes, we have a fair basis upon which to object. This sort of conflict dampening is a big challenge. After all, it's nicer just to be in love, isn't it? But eventually we have to deal with the hard stuff or we can't continue being in love.

On the other hand, there are some couples who make their relationship all work. Utter seriousness and an inability to share good times together should be a red flag. Too much heavy communication and working stuff through is bad — you need some natural harmony here.

Often it's easy to get caught up in the intricacies of relationship impasses without stepping back and assessing the health of what's happening. Do it. Be fair in your assessment of whose baggage is whose, then deliver it to both doorsteps. Usually the problem is either not assuming responsibility, overblaming yourself, or not coming up with alternatives for the future.

Ask yourself, "How do I see the problem? How am I contributing to it?" Then go to your partner with a minimum of hostility and defensiveness. Share your view of things and what you feel is your contribution. Take ten deep breaths, and meanwhile, watch their reaction very carefully. How they respond is your key to weathering this impasse, and others in the future. Don't make a firm decision after only one impasse. One indicator of a person's emotional health is their ability to overcome their own defensiveness and own up to their own mistakes. Actually, this is a healthy way of sticking up for themselves.

Just because you've identified someone's behavior as unhealthy doesn't mean you have to reject that person. Sit down and say, "Look, this is what's happening. I'm not comfortable with it. I would like to look at alternative ways of meeting our needs or dealing with it." On the other hand, if you find yourself doing too much of this, it may be a sign that it's time to cut your losses and get out. Break it off, go home, drink a beer, lick your wounds, and wait a while before calling up your friends and stealing one of their dates. Faced with the accumulation of a bunch of unhealthy interactional patterns, try to assess whether you are a person who stays in relationships too long or quits too early. Try to stretch yourself to go against your first inclinations toward fight or flight.

Honesty versus Privacy versus Secrets

One of the trickier discriminations to make is between appropriate and inappropriate honesty and privacy. Anyone who has ever had a friend "do them a favor" by showering them with "total honesty" knows how obnoxious and destructive this can be. You will occasionally be faced with tricky situations where it's hard to know what to do, what to explain, and what to leave out. As the folk-rock singer Michelle Shocked sings "Silence is golden, words are made of lead/ In the alchemy of love, you know some things are better left unsaid."

Suggestion: accentuate and share the positive, along with *some* of the negative, when you're confident your mood and timing might make such sharing constructive. To use an extreme example, partners usually won't welcome the news that you're lusting after their best friends by saying, "thanks for being honest." Obviously, sharing this information is tacky: keep it private.

However, sleeping with their best friends and lying about it is no longer in the domain of privacy. We all know stuff like this is lousy, but it happens. Transgressions hurt any kind of relationship.

Secrecy and the Infidel

By this point you should have exchanged some of your naivete for savvy, lest you wind up becoming an unwitting
member of that unfortunate group F.C.O.A. (Future Cuck-
olds of America). Take preventive steps: avoid tempting situations. No one dives into the ocean without wading into the
water a ways first. When you feel your feet getting wet, take
a look around at where you are headed. Some couples have
made a pact specifying that before they have an affair, they
have to call their partner first and explain. Agreeing to this
minimizes our regrettable tendency to brainwash ourselves.

Keeping secrets about real transgressions compounds the
hurt and potential for destruction. Secrecy and lying de-
grades the good things you may have had going before the
transgression, like honesty, trust, and openness. As more
time goes by, the relationship becomes more tainted by the
hollowness of the honesty being assured.

Secrets are the emotional equivalent of the Great Wall of
China. They profoundly affect your potential for intimacy.
The deception and false spin that such cover-ups entail in-
troduce confusion and speculation into not only your partner's perceptions about what is really going on with you, but
also into your own ability to be open.

Because secrets and subterfuge give power to those "in-
the-know," they violate a fundamental basis of relationship
health: equality. You have plenty of obstacles to face together as it is. Why muck things up by having anything but
a healthy respect for each other's privacy and a mutual expectation of honesty? In the long term, you injure the vital-
ity and strength of your bond, perhaps irrevocably.

Healthy Strife

Remember, however, that some amount of conflict is normal and healthy. Couples who never fight get at each other in all kinds of much sneakier, more destructive ways by letting grudges build up and then dumping them all at once. If you start having fantasies about how you could change your partner, think of this as a red flag. You're not a saint, so don't feel like you should act like one.

Instead of asking how you can change your partner, ask yourself if you can live with this sort of behavior. This is crucial. Knowing when and how to ask for help is one of the most important skills we can develop as young adults, and this is never more true than when our relationships feel all out of whack.

What I like in a partner is someone who is interesting, who bothers to get to know me well enough to challenge me,

---

☐ Some Relationship Tips

- Life's too short for lousy communication
- Give relationships plenty of time, go at a comfortable pace
- Take a chance on someone beautiful, but go for depth
- Don't marry anyone you haven't broken up with at least a couple of times
- Anger is both the enemy and the brother of passion
- The imagination is a sexual organ
- Court forever
- Observe the "rebound ratio rule." For every year you were involved with someone, wait a month after you break up before seeing someone new
- Same goes for engagements, but try to wait one full year after a serious engagement before seeing someone else seriously

---

and who isn't afraid to tell me when I'm not doing my share of the dishes. How can you grow without someone pointing out the sometimes unpleasant truths about yourself?

The Great Healthy Partner Hunt and Other Traps

Getting solid perspectives on health is complicated by the fact that even basically sound and healthy people get into unhealthy patterns. Health is a battle of sorts because we all have both constructive and destructive impulses. Maintaining some semblance of sanity requires vigilance, clearheadedness, some great toys, and friends who will tell you what they really think. Keep in mind that skirmishes and wrinkles in relationships are inevitable. And if you don't feel like your relationship has any problems, get ready, because perfect couples, like perfect families, often self-destruct in frightening ways.

This is not to condone "the great healthy partner hunt" in too puritanical a way. After all, it's very stimulating being around people with quirks and oddities. The British, for instance, celebrate their eccentrics with a pride bordering on glee. Straight arrows who never take risks and lead Eagle Scout existences usually wind up boring their companions.

The point is, if you're going to be with someone who is more than a little unhealthy, let's hope they're unhealthy in ways you find interesting or even a bit brilliant, but that don't bring you down. Some screwed-up people creatively engage their craziness in such a way that later in life, they sail into a kind of rare maturity, sometimes even a state of grace. Although being together with someone like this involves some ups and downs, there is excitement in watching them unfold. You can get along with some truly screwed-up people (who are destined to remain so or become even worse) if you are careful and guide yourself gracefully through it. Why you would want to, given the number of other cool people around, is another question. Studies of creative people show that they tend to be more open about their craziness than the rest of us. Flirting with the edges of rationality can be both beautiful and nightmarish.

So, who is really healthy anyway? Use common sense here. Stay away from those who might be heavily into drugs, visiting past partners, or those who simply don't have the time to put into a relationship. "Doctors make lousy partners," a female friend concluded after dating a witty medical resident for six months or so, "but it's not their fault, they just don't have the time." Other things to watch out for: people still confused about their sexual orientation or still struggling through a lot of painful issues from the past; people who treat their friends and family poorly; people with no sense of humor or who don't seem to be able to laugh at themselves; people who try to "win" at relationships; people who can't deal with the intensity of resolving some difficult emotional conflict in a relationship; people who have a hard time asking for help. You fill in the rest here.

Ultimately, it's more of a match thing than anything else. If you're a nine-to-five person who loves athletics and has a stressful career, don't try too hard to make things work with an anarchist jazz musician who wakes up to her first cigarette at three in the afternoon and is into paradigms and consciousness.

Hurt

Some people seem prone to getting burned and badly hurt in their twenties. Bad luck and naivete abounds. Oftentimes, we sit around in disbelief after a break-up, muttering over and over, "how did it come apart so soon?" before we find it within ourselves to move on. Emotional pain takes time to heal just like physical pain. We need to lose our innocence about relationships in our twenties or we will constantly set ourselves up for disappointment and betrayal. Getting hurt once should be initiation enough.

Often, as a result of getting hurt, people declare war on the opposite sex. Let's face it, men are basically pigs and women are always the pure, faultless victims of men's swining around. Or is it that women are capricious, manipulative, overly emotional psycho-warriors who screw up the lives of regular, hard-working guys? I can never remember which, but these are the extremes you hear from people venting their spleens.

One sign that you may be making progress is when you get glimpses of the person who, it seems, is becoming less and less the enemy (i.e., the "opposite" sex). Another sign that you're making progress is if instead of whispering "I love you," your partner shouts "Do it to me, baby!" One tires of a lot of meek and tentative groping around.

Sometime in your life, you will be looking at the one you love and will be aware of a shift. Suddenly, you will experience a kind of pure contact with them. I have refrained from the important topic of falling in love because it is so well covered by others. If you're interested in learning more about love from two substantial sources, one is Maggie Scarf's *Intimate Partners*, which is made up of transcriptions of interviews with married couples in therapy. Another excellent resource is entitled *Dreams of Love and Fateful Encounters*, an illuminating, if sometimes dense, scholarly work by the clinical psychiatrist Ethel S. Person. Her lively analysis integrates psychological theory with film, literature, and biographies of many fascinating historical figures. And, best of all, she believes in romantic love as a genuine experience for a significant majority of people.

Is Intimacy Always Short-Lived?

The impermanence of relationships isn't as inevitable as many of us assume. Long-term commitments, believe it or not, can be fun. Lots of people dream of making a lasting commitment to someone — not just someone who'll hold your hand, but someone to be your best friend, dance partner, lover, and parent of your children. Moving in and out of a lot of relationships does get tiring. There's nothing like a little constancy during this time of flux and transition to smooth out the rough patches. Having someone around who really knows you is a definite asset.

The trick is, people have to match up in so many ways to be compatible — intelligence, values, aspirations, lifestyle, cleanliness standards. It isn't the divorce rate that's so amazing; it's the fact that the marriage rate is still so high, that people stick with it, that should astonish us

At any rate, the Nineties are showing signs of serious changes in the rituals of love. People don't propose much anymore, they "discuss getting engaged." Friends say, "Skip the china dude, I want a gift certificate from the hardware store for my wedding." And they get it. Not that any of this is so horrible — it's merely to point out that relationship mores and traditions are changing and evolving all the time.

Intimacy can last, but we have to be willing to work at it. It helps if we can give up unrealistic notions of entitlement regarding our own happiness. Do not feel that you have the right to be happy every minute and that not being happy is good cause to split with a spouse or live-in partner.

I once overheard an intriguing conversation in a local high school in which a trio of girls were discussing how a certain guy would make a great "starter" husband for one of their friends. This way, they agreed, she could have a lot of fun and get some good experience until she needed to move

139

on. Few conversations since have bowled me over quite as much as that one.

One interviewee, a pastor who does divorce counseling, goes home to his wife some nights saying, "If you had divorced me for the reasons she (his client) stated tonight, you would have had to get rid of me seven times." For better or worse, the unhappiness threshold is lower for young people today, and society has promoted this with its focus on instant and continuous gratification. This is a tricky area. One cannot support years of misery just to keep a relationship together. But it does seem like people aren't hanging in there as long as they might, though. As common as divorce is, I don't think anyone should ever see it as a "normal" phenomenon around which to plan one's life and family.

Of course commitment never guarantees the success of a relationship, but it is one of the factors that goes a long way toward assuring it. Sometimes a lighter load seems right for us, relationship-wise, and sometimes we need the major effort that comes with total commitment.

The Leap

Perhaps love's central tension is between the search for perfection and the desire for companionship. The old joke about how the engagement period is the time for the woman to decide whether she can do better has some truth in it for all of us.

Once you make that leap of faith and put all of your eggs in one basket — WATCH THAT BASKET. Until then, it's healthier to cultivate a kind of mutual interdependence with many different friends (read: spreading your eggs around). One important and often overlooked potential benefit to the long-term success of a relationship is community. How many people know both partners and consider them friends? Is there a group that celebrates, works, and provides a reference point for the couple? Such a group can be an enormous stress-absorber.

If and when you are approaching a decision-making point regarding marriage, take a good look at both of your sets of parents and draw some contrasts and comparisons. Many people enter into relationships with the hidden hope of getting something from their partner that they could never get from one parent. This is often a set-up for failure. Such hidden agendas crash because the weight of the need often overwhelms the other partner.

Try to be aware of what you're getting into and take your time. Sound preparation for a long relationship requires time, some good fights, experiencing troubling times together to see how you do, and education. We need to take on the responsibility to educate our partner about how best to communicate and not hit our "hot buttons." For example, this may mean we refrain from yelling because of whatever greater unpleasantness happened in our partner's house when yelling occurred. Or another example might be to not use guilt as a weapon, because if someone was not raised in a home where guilt was a prominent influence tactic, it just appears foolish. Everyone brings some level of emotional conflict to a relationship. We're all working on this stuff all the time. It's just a matter of degree. If you bring many emotional conflicts to a bond, a sick choice of a mate will make for sick results.

It can be a tough call to make, though, when you find someone it really feels right to be with. One couple decided to get married because they figured that if they didn't, one would always get some career offer in some other place and just cruise. They have since done really well. Another couple was at that decision-making moment, decided not to, and are now a little shocked at how little the other person means to them eight months later. So, who knows? You pays your money, you takes your chances.

An older friend feels that one of the keys to knowing if you've met someone you love enough to marry is whether you can envision having, and indeed want to have, children with them. Being compatible is one thing, but ask yourself if you can sincerely hope that your kids turn out like your partner. This is a good indicator of what you sense at unconscious levels about your partner's ability to be both a loving partner and a strong parent. If they pass this test, your family likes your beloved, and you have known each other for at least a year, you may even be ready to go ahead (Yikes!). Unfortunately, the statistics are rather grim for "whirlwind" romances with little lead time into a marriage, and also for couples whose families don't support the choice of partner. The following is a list of some things that are important for people who are in relationships that are preparing to enter the "marriage zone."

☐ It's Important for Relationships that:

- Eye-contact is made consistently
- Truth-telling is expected and practiced
- Partners work well together, i.e. they both get work done with the other one around
- The couple "acts married," like committed, loyal, and rock-solid partners toward each other
- Both partners know whether the other is a pants-before-sox morning person or a sex-before-pants morning person
- There is roughly equal "air time" (talk doesn't center around one partner)
- The couple has ironed out how they will observe holiday rituals
- There are attempts at joint problem-solving and some resolution to the fights you're having
- The partners are good or best friends
- Neither partner engages in public "baby talk"
- The couple could survive twenty-four hours together at home with no structured activities whatsoever

---

By the way, the "twenty-four-hour test" is no joke. One seasoned premarital counselor had all his couples do this before going ahead with their wedding plans, with bizarre and often hilarious results. Couples entering counseling droolingly in love sometimes wound up celebrating the beginning of a beautiful friendship. Dating is fun, but it is also a famously unreliable means of testing longer-term compatibility. This is because it's structured around leisure, in radical contrast to marriage or family life.

Obviously there is a lot more to the health of relationships than the short list above. For instance, a college friend of mine once argued that you aren't truly in love unless you can pick your partner's nose. Everybody has their own criteria.

Let's Make A Deal

Another key to longevity in relationships is learning to negotiate and make deals. Of course communication is critical to this process, but negotiating deals requires a lot more than mere ease of expression. Solutions to conflicting interests are sometimes hard to come by. Often times one partner winds up doing a bit more to "take care" of the other partner. This is one of a host of potential inequalities that virtually always spell trouble for couples. Such couples need to get better at putting it all on the table, especially the "caretaking" person. It's no time to be bashful and unassertive when it comes to getting these things out in the open.

The more clearly partners can understand what's important to each other, the better they will be able to navigate through the bad patches. Sometimes people are scared off by the feeling that if they voiced all of their needs they would be overwhelmed. The point is, couples don't need to fulfill each other's every need to survive. The cultural notion that marriage is about one person who can fulfill all of your needs all of the time is dangerously misleading. Couples need friends and community to support, enjoy, and challenge each other.

When needs are on the table they can be negotiated according to what seems fair, equal, and possible. The couple can make decisions about what needs they can try to meet. If both partners have a strong interest in getting something from the relationship then something can usually be worked out. You'd be surprised at how much people are willing to give in return for the assurance of getting what they want, be it support, a soft touch, or even the less consequential stuff.

The key here is how good a "deal-maker" you can become. This requires you to make adjustments to changing circumstances. As relationships evolve, needs change. In this way marriage can be seen as a succession of "contracts" that evolve just as the husband and wife evolve.

The point is we're not given much to go on in this department. No one can foresee the kind of person they will be in ten years. It used to be that gender structured the kind of deals you made. These are no longer so entrenched. And with all the fuzzy areas of gender flexibility in terms of who does what in a Nineties household, this can be a confusing and challenging area.

A study that looked at what people valued in their relationships as they looked back on the different stages of their lives found that humor moved from eighth place to first place over the course of life. Intuitively it makes sense to say that humor is just about as important as love. When you think back on the good times you have shared with someone, the laughs are what stand out.

In sum, problematic and frustrating as they are, relationships have the capacity to make your twenties some of the best years of your life. We'll never be as free to pursue them — and fail at them — as we will in our twenties.

EIGHT

Moving Back Home

IT's happening all over. Because young people are either too poor, can't find work, or are trying to save, they are testing to see how far the old umbilical cord will stretch. Some studies show that as many as 40 percent of men aged under thirty-five live at home, and the numbers are only slightly less among women.

As with any mass migration, there are multiple causes and effects at work here: housing costs, the pathetic state of entry-level salaries, parents' need for care or company, the list goes on. As one happy mother put it, "I'd kick 'em out, but it's just that they're such good cooks. . . "

The benefits are obvious: cheap room and board is a major boon to a young person's quality of life. The drawbacks? It may have been awhile since you shared a phone, or had to wait to use one. Old family hassles may flare up again. Anytime you live with people you have to get the ground rules straight. But what new rules should be established? We can't be as free as we were in college, but a return to our high school curfew? Wrong. Discuss things in the open and try to arrive at some mutually satisfying arrangement regarding rules.

Controversies emerge. One guy moved back home so he could save money and immediately started buying components for an ultra high-tech stereo system. His mother was not so sanguine. "We had to struggle for fifteen years before we got some nice stereo equipment. Why should I break my ass just to make it easy on him?" This raises the important issue of use versus abuse. What's fair? What obligations do we have to each other? If someone is just being lazy and really doesn't need the extra help with finances, staying at home may actually be undercutting their momentum. It's harder to get out into the stream of things when you're roosting in your parents' little nest. What is an appropriate reason for moving back home for a spell and what isn't? These are questions our nation is attempting to answer, one family at a time. The questions we have at a more practical level may still nag at us: how will we get along now? What about my social life? What'll my coworkers think of my situation? What if I want that special someone to stay over?

Every family's cultural heritage will entail a different set of norms regarding "boomerangs" — adults kids who return to the nest. In many Mediterranean homes, kids move out of the home when they marry, and sometimes not even then. Other families take in the welcome mat at eighteen, or right after college. Large families often have a kid or two in transition — just divorced, maybe in between jobs — floating through the family homestead at any given point in time. Others have kids who barely set foot in the same state.

There is no one "right" way to make the transition to living at home again. So, improvise and make the best of a situation that is probably ideal for no one but which can furnish some surprising satisfactions. This means negotiation, compromise, and sensitivity.

A piano tuner I interviewed in Chicago found this out the summer he came home from his first year of college: "I went out for a walk on the beach until two in the morning, only to come home to find our house all lit up with a police car in the driveway. My family had been up half the night searching for me." Be sensitive to the fact that your moving home is an adjustment not just for you but for your folks. "When my youngest brother moved out of our home and Mom and Dad were left alone, I was worried that they might be lonely," a free-lance editor and writer related. "My worry was unfounded. Shoot, they socialized more, went on more vacations, and went out to eat, which we never did before because we have a huge family. Whenever I called up my dad and asked him what he was doing, he replied, 'Oh, just chasing your mother around the house.' None of us moved back home, but I'm sure if we had we would have put a crimp into my parents' new lifestyle."

Another important issue that young people struggle with is the negative stigma that sometimes surrounds moving back home. "Some people I meet just don't know what to think at all," a high school teacher who lives at home recounted. "When they hear I live at home they ask, 'what are you, gay or something?' when really it's just that my teaching contract and my lease weren't in sync."

Moving home is O.K. Really, it is an incredible luxury — a cultural aberration — that we live in a society wealthy enough to support all of these independent households. Now we're getting used to the way the rest of the world lives for a change.

If moving back home isn't "normal," however, in terms of your family's cultural background, then I counsel caution. This type of situation is more like a business contract that should feature agreement between two fully informed parties. I strongly suggest that you agree on several issues with your parents right up front and actually draw up a contract and sign it. Make sure the contract includes a specific plan for getting out on your own, i.e. "Joe will move when he saves x amount of money or in one and a half years, whichever comes first." This will save you hassles on down the road when Joe doesn't manage to save as much as he planned and everyone is wondering what they should do. It's not that such a contract should remain inflexible — needs and situations change. But all parties should have a clear understanding of what each other's expectations are. Make sure the contract specifies your duties — mowing the lawn, cooking twice a week, or whatever. Set up periodic meetings with your folks to review how both of you are feeling about the arrangements in the contract, if it feels necessary.

I hate to say it, but if you move back home, your parents are doing extra duty. You are a guest, and I strongly recommend that you make your presence as easy on your parents and other family members as possible. Be an asset. Offer to help drop off cars to be fixed, pick up people from the airport, or do a quick shopping trip when everyone else seems too busy. Try to set things up so that everyone enjoys your presence. And if they want you in a different room than your old one because they have it set up as a study or sitting room, don't make a stink.

There are other concrete things to be mindful of. Act like a roommate and not a kid; resist slipping into old patterns. One good way to insure this is to do your own laundry and iron your own clothes. Another thing you can do is pay rent and some money for food, regardless of what that figure is. This also serves to keep you mindful of outside responsibilities — that everyone else in the world has a rent bill due each month.

Some issues are "hot" with our parents during this time. Money is almost always an issue. I encourage you to become financially independent as soon as you can. If you have to ask them for money, save it for the big stuff like education or weddings, as opposed to new cars, CD players, or vacations. If you accept a lot of money from your parents, you are cutting them in on your "board of directors." In other words, they have a say in your future plans. Don't forget this crucial tradeoff.

Get interested in things outside of your home. This is probably the single most important piece of advice I can give on living at home. It's crucial that you maintain friendships and outside interests. Don't spend too many evenings flipping through the TV channels with your folks. This takes the pressure off your relationship with them. "We come from an old world Eastern European family," a recent college grad working as a translator told me. "It feels pretty normal to be at home, and I have been able to save for graduate school. Me and my brother formed a jazz band together and I really think that having that focus keeps the house pretty sane." Try to retain the trappings of independence even if you don't feel particularly self-sufficient. Also: work. Or barring that, look for work. If someone isn't working, in school, or looking for work it's pretty hard to feel that they aren't abusing the privilege of living at home. It shouldn't be a vacation.

And some seemingly mundane but important technical tips: spring for a separate phone line if your business or social life dominates your parents' phone. This too can relieve some of the pressure of overcrowding. Invest in a good pair of stereo earphones. Let your parents deal with the empty-nest syndrome on their own. This is not a time for you to try to protect them from the inevitable. You've probably got enough to deal with in your own life. Besides, they're tough enough to handle it — they raised you, didn't they?

My parents had to boot me out of the house one spring when I was at my wit's end. I credit them with the eventual independence I secured. But barring divorce, mental illness, physical incapacity, or the need to care for your parents, I will go out on a limb here and say that anyone who is thirty and still lives at home is not trying as hard as they should. It's O.K. not to have found your niche yet as long as you don't make the couch your substitute niche. There are alternatives. You don't *have* to have your own place. At some point it's better to bunk in with three or four people in an apartment rather than live at home.

"Where did I go wrong?" a woman with three grown sons at home pleaded with me. They only work part-time at a local pub, laze around the house all day, and have no plans to move out. In my view she went wrong by not kicking them out. In our society parents have done their duty by the time you are either through college or turn twenty. The rest is gravy. In my opinion she should give them two months, stop doing their laundry and cooking, and kick 'em out.

Then again, many single parents report that they like the idea of at least one of their kids staying home for awhile — the company's good for them. This is fine too as long as the kids like being there and don't feel held back.

Getting Along with Your Parents

Much of how you get along with your parents depends on what your relationship was like before. Get reacquainted. Try to be open-minded. Getting to know your parents as adult friends can be very gratifying. When I think about what I've learned about my parents over the last two years it amazes me how three people living in the same house for so long could not have known so many important things about each other. So listen to your parents carefully.

I myself learned some interesting things about why my own father chose his line of work. It turns out that he had worked at over twenty different jobs by the time he finished college — as a lumberjack, heating oil hauler, cookware salesman, brine-shrimp collector, mechanic, carpenter, and radio disc jockey, among others. Some of these jobs were under work place conditions so harsh (both safety-wise and in terms of poor management relations) that he vowed that he would try to improve the work places of others. He has since become an organizational psychologist doing consulting work with groups ranging from the executive teams of major industries, personnel departments, and factory workers, to state government administrators and prison guards.

At any rate, when it comes to getting along with our parents in our twenties, there is so much to discover about them that it can almost be like becoming friends with people you met long ago and have almost forgotten. Take advantage of the opportunity.

150

A Note on Visiting Home

Interesting as getting reacquainted with our parents as adults can be, we would do well to be cautious about several things if we *don't* live at home. I don't know why it's such a magical number, but many of the people I interviewed reported that three days is the ideal length of a visit with their parents. Of course this depends on the kind of relationship you had with them before. Many people get along fabulously with their folks and consider them their best friends. Others, unfortunately, don't.

Some people said that they learned early on to bring a buffer home with them in the form of a friend or significant other. This allows you to see your parents through different eyes. Oftentimes when we go home alone we get sucked right into playing our part in old family patterns: black sheep, family hero, class clown, marriage counselor, they all get tired pretty quick. Bringing a friend changes the tenor of one's family tune and can help you resist this.

It's O.K. to avoid visiting your parents if you just can't stand being around them. Boycott has a long history as a useful tactic in the face of poor and unfair treatment. As one woman said, "It's never too late to have an adolescent rebellion." She was always the "good kid," and it wasn't until her twenty-seventh year that she was able to go out and have a little fun by, as she put it, "getting a little dangerous."

Mutual Education

Because being young is so different now than it was even twenty years ago, we could all benefit from a little two-way education. Many of our parents had fewer life options and pretty much knew what they had to do when they became adults. Just as a small example, one sixtysomething man told me, "When I had saved enough money to buy a car I had three choices, Ford, Chevrolet or Dodge. Young people now have fifty choices."

For women, becoming an adult meant getting married and having a family. They might have become teachers, nurses, or secretaries. For men, it meant perhaps doing military service, getting some training or maybe going to college, finding a mate, and then going to work for some big company. In one sense this made it easier for them in that they didn't have to do a lot of confusing soul-searching and make the confusing choices that we do. But obviously they were also limited in terms of what options they had. Don't be afraid to let your parents know how difficult you might be finding it to cope with the many choices now confronting you.

Another important issue it's useful to discuss is different values. One woman was talking with her father about what to do with a small inheritance she had received. She was thinking about getting a new potter's wheel (a sometime hobby/occupation for her) or doing some travelling. He said, "Oh, you'd be better off getting a new wheel instead of spending it on a vacation." To her, travel is an educational experience and an important part of becoming the kind of person she values. To him, it's just a vacation.

Parents need to know that it might take longer for twentysomething people to finish their educations and find meaningful work than it took them. Perhaps the cruelest joke played on our generation is the general belief that if you went to college, you'll get a good job and be upwardly mobile.

There has to be some balancing here. What is a realistic timetable for us to get out on our own, and what is unacceptable, especially if one is living at home or relying on the folks for major financial support? Plan a discussion of these things with your parents and get it out in the open. We all have hidden generational assumptions that we often don't articulate

152

even for ourselves, yet they play a huge role in how we think about, plan, and live our lives. It's nice to have people around who are concerned enough about you to crack the whip from time to time. Sometimes we need to set some goals and give our lives more structure so that we can avoid becoming aimless.

As one man said, "I was passed over for promotion at one point and came home for a few weeks. I felt like quitting my job. I really expected my folks to be disappointed and angry but really they just wanted me to feel O.K. about myself. There was no big pressure to be a big success or anything. They just wanted me feeling O.K., and that gave me the boost I needed to get back in there and give it another shot."

Dealing With Your Demons

One difficult issue that can crop up is painful memories we may have towards an abusive or neglectful parent. It's important to respect our feelings about these experiences. There's no sin in having negative feelings towards our parents if they are grounded in real events. Respecting one's own hurt and anger is the only way to heal them. Some people send their parents their therapy bills. Others invite them into a family session when they are ready to confront and heal their old wounds.

The benefits of this type of reconciliation are enormous. You *can* quell your old demons. Although cutting off can be a very functional solution for a while, eventually we must face the music and learn to reconnect with our family if we want to spare ourselves a lot of psychic anguish — and spare our children a similar fate. As one interviewee said, "My sister has this intense bitterness towards our mom, and although I think it was appropriate years ago, I wish she could just let go and get on with it." Dealing with a problematic parent relationship can be frustrating and trying during these years, sometimes the most trying aspect of our lives. But they should definitely benefit from some work on your part. I would highly recommend not living at home if you are still caught up in some emotionally difficult issues with your parents.

Welcome to the world of the Boomerang. Life back home can be fraught with pitfalls and delights for all parties involved. Negotiation, compromise, and sensitivity will serve you well as you tiptoe back and forth across the threshold of independence.

NINE

Confusion

Confusion. What a pal. He usually brings his unwelcome buddies lethargy, aimlessness, and the blues to your self-pity parties as well. If you're not careful, they will drink all the liquor in the house.

When asked what advice he had for people in their twenties, one forty-year-old chiropractor replied, "You know, I was so out of it, so lost, I don't feel like I should say anything." When the people I interviewed in researching this book were asked to reflect on their twenties, many of them spoke in this manner. They were just glad they got through it and sometimes marvelled at how they managed at all. Confusion is a major culprit. Sometimes we just don't have enough information about ourselves and the world until we're into our thirties.

Confusion as a Process of Elimination

Confusion can be chronic during the twenties. Sometimes we don't know what we need to know to climb out of the valley; other times we know, but we're stalling. Writing has been known to help clarify lots of things. Stop whining to your friends and whine to a journal. Above all, if you are confused, then go ahead and be confused. It's not the confusion itself that trips people up, it's the feeling that being confused somehow isn't O.K. and that they shouldn't be feeling it.

But do try to do something about your confusion. Half of the battle in figuring out what you want is figuring out what you don't want. That's why trying anything can help — the way out of confusion is often a slow process of elimination.

Seldom do the clouds part and the birds sing and everything becomes sweetness and light. It can take time, work, and the achievement of a perspective for which we're not quite ready. After the fact, you may feel that some of what you were confused about was useful while some of it was just spinning circles around yourself. This is normal. Personal lives, as much as we'd like them to, do not function according to laws of efficiency and optimization; sometimes our troubles are caused by thinking they somehow should. Usually we have good reason to be confused, and yet, after the fact, one is often left with a sense of wasted time. Remember that there is nothing new in the history of Western civilization about wasting time.

Keep in mind that all decisions involve limited knowledge, unforseen boons and drawbacks, and tradeoffs. Unfortunately, many people put off tough choices because they do not want to face the tradeoff. Somehow they figure that if they don't decide they will magically get the best of both worlds. This is malarkey. Strive to cut those magical elements out of your thinking. The price you pay for putting off such tough choices can be great. When you have gathered a fair amount of information about the choices you perceive in front of you, and then brainstormed a few more, push yourself to make a choice. This is what grown-ups do, as well as leaders in every field. You'll be wrong sometimes, but that's better than not being anything.

Roping Bull at the New Age Rodeo

There's a lot of New Age bull floating around out there that many people are mistaking for useful information about how to resolve their life quandaries. Many of these reconstructed hippies, cranks, and pseudo-mystics who push this stuff prey on the confused. Beware of people with the kind of earnestness that's painful to be around. This earnestness floats around in the form of books, workshops, and inspirational tapes.

Demand from yourself some sharp observations about the meaning of your confusion. Crystals won't get you out of an interpersonal jam no matter how big they are. Whatever you do, don't give into idiotic platitudes like "it was all meant to be, all part of what I needed to be learning on my path," or "I'm really glad I lost that job because now I see that I created that loss so that I could have this incredible new awareness." You are more original than that. Use your brain instead of shoehorning your experience into facile cliches.

The college roommate of a friend of mine advised him that there was a "deeper meaning" behind the loss of his cassette tape collection on a plane ride home. Somehow this must mean, his roommate reflected, that he was ready for a new stage in his "spiritual unfolding." After meditating on this for awhile, the tape-loss victim discovered that this "deeper meaning" involved a fast-talking huckster at the airport in between flights who hustled him. That was the last time he remembered having his cassette case. About five minutes later he realized it was gone. This "deeper meaning" wasn't exactly what his roommate had in mind.

New Age approaches to spirituality have recently become terribly lopsided towards the positive. Ten years ago, the emphasis on being a seeker of knowledge and recognizing that we sometimes needlessly create problems for ourselves was beneficial. Somewhere along the line, however, the distinction between self-created pain and natural, important pain was lost. Whatever happened to being able to recognize that we are unhappy without trying to plaster it over with a lot of overly positive brainwashing? Sometimes life hurts. It's important to run the full gamut of your emotions without prematurely giving in to that cold voice that says, "O.K., you've had a good cry, now it's time to get on with your life."

The power of accurate thinking is always more useful than the power of positive (or cynical) thinking.

When one looks back on one's life, it's hard to be convinced that everything one went through was useful, educational, and necessary. Whenever we are truly torn and confused about an important relationship or geographical move it means we are in a sort of limbo. There is anxiety and discomfort involved in making choices and struggling with how we go about making major life decisions. Suffering, although it can be a great teacher, is also sometimes arbitrary and without larger meaning. This is where I part company with M. Scott Peck in his otherwise superb book, *The Road Less Travelled*, where he (among other things) expertly establishes the links between spirituality and mental health. One of his main ideas — that the avoidance of suffering in the journey of life is more of a problem than the suffering itself — is a sound and important principle. I would like to humbly add, though, that suffering, however bravely met, does not always reward us with poignant insight and new ways to cope. Nevertheless, this is a worthwhile read. His emphasis on discipline as a way out of much of life's difficulty is brilliant.

We all like to pretend that hope springs eternal, that society, despite its rough edges, is basically fair, and that sex is all about pleasure and nothing about power. Guess what? It's time we lift some of those veils in terms of how we look at our own lives.

Genuine growth does not tend to follow neat patterns. Much of what we endure is not useful to us later. Generation and decay are sometimes indistinguishable.

Deeper Meanings

Meet your suffering as gracefully and bravely as you can and do not expect more than humble rewards. As the protagonist (played by Bill Murray) in the film *The Razor's Edge* says after he loses the love of his life, "You learn that you don't get rewarded for leading a good life." Keeping this in mind might allow you to be pleasantly surprised by the rewards you reap from suffering instead of enduring even more disillusionment.

Try to maintain a healthy balance of both growth and stability in your life. Confusion increases the temptation to become an "experience junkie" by running from one supposed enlightenment fix to another in the flaky trot of the New Age neurotic. Because of the confusing array of choices and lack of certainties that our generation faces, many of us fall prey to joining cults and making intense commitments to groups that purport to do our thinking for us. The danger is that they may reshape us in artificial ways. Many of the people in my interviews described this as being a typical rite of passage in their twenties, whether it be submersion in the New Age, excessive therapy, or aikido.

Confusion as Invitation

Confusion is often a healthy invitation to work on building more clarity in our lives. Often people get confused when they have too many options, or too few. Try to get these numbers into a manageable range. Whenever you are confused about an upcoming transition, write letters to old friends. This in itself can be useful therapy. You'll be amazed at what you can learn just by listening to yourself talk. It is an excellent way to explore your reactions to and reflections on your life. The writing process allows you to relate different people, themes, and patterns to different levels of consciousness and memory, and helps to integrate your experience of them.

Do a little research about what it is you don't know. Pay close attention to yourself. Hang out with people who seem to really know what they're doing and study them. Being confused can be good if you continue to learn. If you are so confused you are immobile, seek help. This can really work if you find a competent and caring therapist you like. Don't be shy about asking for help when you need it. Finances are really no object. Many therapists and agencies operate on a sliding scale; it's more a matter of finding one you're comfortable with.

Good Confusion

I am a firm believer in good confusion. Sometimes it would be very wrong not to be at all confused about something. Sometimes we need to sort through our values, our commitments, and our relationships and especially their "shadow" sides in order to arrive at more fruitful perspectives. Time taken to seek out new dynamic directions is well worth it. Bounce your confusions off of friends to help you get a clearer picture of the issues. Even if they seem muddled in ambiguity, you at least get to find a position amidst the confusion. As one fiftysomething man reported after first leaving his professorship, then establishing a successful business, and then leaving it, "Well, you're always somewhere. The universe does provide that for you, even if that position isn't clear to you yet." He had spent a lot of time casting about for what to do next but was able to come up with that insight despite his feelings of being adrift.

The basic difference between good confusion and bad is this. Good confusion is when you know you are confused and adjust your approach accordingly. Bad confusion is when you aren't aware you are confused and go on acting as though you aren't. A woman confidently told friends and family that she wanted to settle down and marry her boyfriend. But he had his doubts. To hear him tell it, she kept flirting at bars, calling up old boyfriends, and standing

him up. Eventually, she ran off with a guy going to mortu-
ary school somewhere in Massachusetts. She is going to hurt
more people before she's through if she doesn't come to terms
with her ambivalence and confusion. A guy who says he isn't
sure he wants to settle down right away might hurt the
woman in his life who is ready to settle, but at least he's willing to admit his ambivalence. This couple may yet get somewhere out of this good confusion.

Remember that if you didn't get confused once in a while,
you would have a hopelessly simple world view. Oftentimes
after severe bouts of confusion, people experience a reaffir-
mation of old values that have come into question.

Depression

In my capacities as both a therapist-in-training and a friend,
I have seen a lot of people go through hard times in their
twenties. In researching this book, I spoke with the following: people who spent eight years trying to get into medical
school and still didn't make it; a guy who became so committed to radical politics that his relationships with his family
and friends fell apart; several people whose promising relationships were scorched by sexual manipulation and dis-
honesty; people who took nine years to get through college
because their families were so crazy, or who had to work
that long just to pay for it. I heard reminiscences about debilitating drug habits, slumlords, unsafe sex, homelessness,
and hospital corridors that lock behind you.

Because of my exposure to such stories (most of which
were not this grim) I am unable to dismiss this period as
merely a "transition to adulthood." It is too bizarre and interesting and scary to be summed up so neatly.

At some point in your life you're going to lose someone
close, or suffer some accident of fate, or you're going to feel
all out of whack for no discernible reason. What do you do

when the Voice of Doom parks his boom-box in your subcranial membrane? That's when you're going to need to reach out to God, a healing friendship, anything. Research reports that one in ten Americans will suffer a "clinical depression" (read: nasty) during their lifetimes, but the other nine will probably nod to themselves upon hearing Baudelaire's line, "I have felt the wind of the wing of madness." Depression exists on a continuum, and everyone experiences theirs in different ways.

Once your struggle has begun, it can feel like there's not much you can do except ride it out as best you can. Just cope, struggle, and muddle your way through. But it gets better, it really does, and there are things you can do to help. As one woman interviewed for this book put it, "I didn't enter my twenties having a perspective on where I was going. Nothing has really turned out the way I thought it would. There's been a lot more pain to get through than I ever thought humanly possible."

One of the central goals behind this book has been to encourage you to take steps to prevent hard times. Each of us has some control over how tough those inevitable tough times become. However, once they're rolling, it can feel like there are no simple solutions.

Gather supportive friends and family around you and let them in on your troubles. Get the help you need, but be careful not to burn out your support system. Seek out people who are better at listening than at giving advice. Advice is often made to make the giver feel helpful, an expression of what they wish they had done, or a projection onto their own messes. Be sure to continue attending social activities, family events, and spending time on your hobbies, even if you don't feel like you're much fun. One man put it this way: "There was one summer when I was twenty-three that was particularly troubling, when I found myself having difficulty just hanging on. I'd never felt that way before. Sometimes when I was most afraid I was coming apart I would call up one of my friends and ask if I could come over for awhile. When I got there I wouldn't pour out all my troubles and problems. The point was to feel regular again, like the old me. And that's why this worked pretty well — we would do and talk about the regular things in the regular way. This helped me get my perspective back, and put me on more solid ground."

Hope

When you feel a depression coming on, work hard at retaining hope. The famous Japanese filmmaker Akira Kurosawa once said that the struggle to maintain hope is the greatest human struggle. Hope can come from curious sources: kittens, a poem, the newspaper, a walk in the country. Be open to them. Try to keep in mind, implausible as this may seem at the time, that people often look back on their toughest times as periods of intense growth. You might be learning things that will take on useful meaning to you only years (and I mean *years*) later. Hope helps to organize your latent resources.

Psychotherapy is an option to consider. The ability to recognize when we're in a little over our heads and to have the maturity to ask for help is a crucial skill. It's certainly helped me and many of the people I interviewed get through some stormy passages. If we can get over the initial feeling of shame (or sense that we are somehow admitting that we can't do it alone) in asking for help from a counselor, we are affirming a less ego-driven concern for our well-being. For despite the emphasis placed on going it alone in our culture, if we want to "go it" at all well, we will benefit greatly from including others in that process.

Many adults, having had a good first experience with therapy, return when they find themselves getting stuck. It's like a 10,000-mile check-up on your car. One learns that it's better to check it out and get some situations fixed before the stress and danger increases our risk for accidents.

You Owe it To Yourself

Finally, having to suffer through some bad times, you owe it to yourself to get through it so that you know that you can bounce back. Stick it out. Knowing what it's like to bounce back from a horrible episode — affirmation of your resilience — is a valuable gift. It puts more trivial stresses and cares in their proper perspective.

Most of my interviewees reported feeling less vulnerable to everyday stresses as time went on. What's a little poverty after what you've been through? What's a little job-stress? These things lose their power to throw you off balance. Stress consultants say that there are two basic laws: first, don't sweat the little stuff, and second, it's all little stuff.

When you come out of a tough time, you become a community resource. Many of the people I interviewed reported that after a going through some personal troubles, they better appreciated the importance of being a support for other people. After a difficult period people often glide right into functioning as a sort of natural "listening post" in their community. Be there for friends, especially if others have been there for you.

A Short List

Here is a short list of what many people have found helps them when circumstances become bigger than people. (I also recommend David Burns's book for overcoming depression, *Feeling Good: The New Mood Therapy*.)

Exercise Getting up and going really helps. Physical exertion can wash the impurities you're experiencing out of your system. Oftentimes, we quit exercising before we benefit because we defeat ourselves mentally. I find that I forget my troubles more, and get more exercise, when I play team sports like basketball. That way, you lose yourself in the game. So don't just sweat; sweat like a pig.

Change Your Focus Develop some strategies to break your focus on the negative. Get up, move around, force yourself to think about white elephants instead. Read a magazine, shine your shoes, take a long walk by the water. Walk until you feel better. If you don't feel better, walk until you're so tired you can't wait to go home and collapse from exhaustion. Or lock yourself in a room with five trashy novels and don't emerge until you've read them all. Forget any previous literary or aesthetic standards.

Do Things That Make Yourself Feel Useful It's important to engage in useful activities so that you can retain some shreds of self-respect. They can be simple. While you're at work, fake business-as-usual. The routine will help you feel more normal and comfortable and prevent even more stress from further disrupting whatever you're going through. Try not to betray what's really going on with you at your work place; save this topic for friends. While away from work, structure your evenings with basic tasks: cleaning your bird feeder, sweeping the porch, or organizing your books and records. Do whatever you can to remain as independent and busy as possible.

Develop a Crush on Someone No kidding. Sometimes the thrill of such harmless but charming possibilities is a fun escape. Crushes and romance can divert you when you need to be diverted. You don't have to do anything special to enjoy that ticklish buildup of tension and the sweet anticipation of seeing that potential love object during the day. Even if you would never conceivably act on it.

Listen to a Lot of Coltrane or Joni Mitchell, or your favorite old Beatles records, Bach, or whatever. Sometimes music can speak to your healing mechanisms better than you can.

Notice the Good Gather around yourself images of the not-so-awful things in your life and tape them to your forehead. Learn to identify and put a halt to cynical thoughts. There are wonderfully goofy, hysterical things going on in the world. Don't miss out on them for long.

Do Something for Someone Else Helping others is a great way to avoid self-pity. Make a card, run an errand, or offer to take care of a friend's pet for a weekend while they're away.

Give Yourself an Out Plan an escape. One summer while I was in college I went out to Cape Cod on a lark. But once I arrived there were problems: plenty of cheesy jobs but little affordable housing. I called and made a plane reservation home just in case I couldn't find something soon and immediately felt better. As it turned out I found a great place two days later. If your current housing situation is stressful, check into moving in with a friend for awhile: contemplation of this option can release pressure. Of course, don't follow through impulsively.

What to Do if You're Completely and Utterly Depressed Take a part-time job at a stand-up comedy club, listen to all of the acts, stare blankly ahead at all times, and whatever you do, don't laugh. Many depressed people report that they cannot experience pleasure. Therefore you must make extra efforts to find enjoyment and relief from oppressive thoughts. Get a bunch of magazines, cut out all the eyes and noses, and make a collage. Dance with a lamp shade on your head.

Stigma

One of the toughest by-products of going through a tough time is the social stigma that sometimes surrounds you. People who are visibly suffering from a mental illness or a tough time can be scary to other people. Our trials make them confront the fact that this could happen to them. Keep in mind that everyone knows someone who has been touched by mental disability. It's the biggest secret going. Every closet has skeletons.

How to deal with blatant stigma? Carry yourself with dignity. Do not feel a need to explain yourself and only do so on your own terms. A bright young man raced through his pre-med undergrad program with top marks until there was a divorce in his family. He took it hard, and as time went on his grades dipped and he stopped seeing friends. Basically he kind of flipped out. Eventually, he checked himself into a psychiatric program because of his inability to keep functioning. When he left after a month or so, he followed up with counseling and started applying to med schools. How to explain himself to admission committees was a tricky question, but he decided to come clean. As it turned out there was some debate about his fitness for the stresses of medicine, but the committee decided that his seemed to be an acute episode and that here clearly was a person who knew when he needed help. This fact recommended him to the committee. He was admitted to a prestigious school not because he was a superstar but because he did what he needed to do to get himself through a hard time. It's nice to think that at least in some pockets of the world, such even-handedness and lack of fear exists.

Stigma is the result of fear and lack of education. Try to get together with family and friends who were affected by your down time and educate each other about how you reacted. This minuscule swallowing of pride will open the way for them to see that you care about how you affect others. Most of all, don't be too paranoid about it. After you get to know enough people in life you realize that everyone has "issues" of one kind or another.

The stigma associated with being blue can cut you to the quick long after your difficult time is over. As the noted psychiatrist Karl Menninger once said, "I am a bleeding heart.

I see lots of things to bleed about." Life can take tragic turns, and we would do well to keep this in mind before we judge others too quickly or too harshly.

Who You Are

Don't ask. Sorry, I mean ask, but don't get obsessed. Maintain a wholesome interest in yourself. Chances are you won't really have a good sense of who you are until you've been out in the world for a few years anyway. Besides, you're always adding new parts. The Buddhists say that any fixed conception of self is a convenient fiction. So, inconvenience yourself. Try to incline yourself less toward soul-digging (the burrowing-deep-in-order-to-find-your-real-self plan) than toward leading the unpredictable life (getting out there, bumping up against life for awhile, and learning from doing). You really don't want to recognize yourself too readily at each new stage.

Identity is a strange admixture of work and accident. It seldom crystallizes without effort and expression. It's like clay: you can sit and stare at it or you can spin it on a wheel, add some glaze, and maybe fire it in a kiln. Sculptures are usually a little more interesting than lumps of stared-at clay. Extricate your identity from convention. It's hard to understand yourself in a vacuum, so do so in terms of your relationships with your friends, your family, and your art. Everyone has a spark of creativity that they bring to some area of their lives, no matter how hard they try to closet it away.

One thing that makes it difficult to admit to being depressed in our culture is the American faith in self-improvement. The socially and morally reinforced pursuit of happiness is the real American rat race. Take a look at the throngs lining up at your neighborhood New Age bookstore. This should be evidence enough of how unrelenting our efforts have become to cram our lives full of contentment. We get tired of smiling. To admit to our despair is almost like admitting to failure. It is as if we are saying that there is something wrong with us if we can't manufacture our own happiness.

Twentysomething Risks

One could argue that we are actually more at risk in our twenties than during other life-stages because our mistakes have real-world consequences for our employability, sanity, and our relationships. Some evidence of the risks we run has been outlined in recent public health figures on suicide. The suicide rate for fifteen- to nineteen-year-olds is one of the highest in history. The fact that this suicide rate actually doubles for twenty- to twenty-four-year-olds almost defies comprehension. This is little-known data. Moreover, medical experts project that between now and the year 2000, the heaviest increase in the suicide rate will also be in this same early-twenties age group. This is an emergency. We need to take a closer look at what's really going on with people so we can help them step back from the brink. As a social worker put it: "My experience has been that most of the people who were suicidal at one time are glad they didn't do it. Whatever their problems were, they tended to work themselves out, or at least they felt better at coping with them. Most of them go on to have very satisfying lives."

Medical research indicates that young adults are especially vulnerable to emotional and mental disorders. One of the largest of these studies shows that the average age at which major anxiety disorders appear is nineteen; drug abuse, twenty; alcoholism, twenty-three; and depressive disorders, twenty-five. Schizophrenia typically emerges in the late teens and early twenties. We are at risk for developing some of the most debilitating, disruptive, and scary illnesses there are. With the exception of phobias, which seem to appear in childhood, this period is a virtual mine field for mental and emotional problems. Sixty-year-old men sometimes make macabre jokes about their approach to "heart attack alley," the time when they are most likely to suffer a heart attack or stroke. Based on this evidence, we can generally say that for us this is "angst alley."

This data illustrates why a film like *Ordinary People* was so powerful. It showed what to all appearances seemed to be a typical upper-middle-class family experiencing a lot of hidden distress. Since the death of his brother, the teenage son struggles with depression, suicide, and making sense of his parents chilly marriage. It made what in clinical terms might be called a "mental disorder" seem very normal, and gave it a human face. All families go through difficult and sad times together at some point. This film affirmed the normality of this kind of seeming "abnormality" because the son's reactions seem like an appropriate response to his circumstances. The therapist is portrayed as competent and caring, a fresh surprise considering the usual monsters that inhabit Hollywood efforts. As the film closes we have a sense the son is going to make it, although we know his problems aren't over yet.

Remember that these types of conditions can be extremely disruptive, so we can assume that the person who begins to experience a major depression at nineteen continues to deal with its after-effects for years beyond its initial onset. Many substance-abuse counselors tell their chemically dependent clients that they should expect about two years of hard work on their lives before they are back on track. Please don't conclude from all of this that therefore we all pretty much need professional help. We don't. But there are probably some of us who could benefit from talking to someone from time to time, especially if we feel like things are taking a turn for the worse. If you're unsure, ask a friend.

The Howling Tempest

The noted American author William Styron (*Sophie's Choice*) feels the word "depression" is a half-assed, wimpy word for what is really a "howling tempest in the brain." He describes its manifestations excruciatingly well — the crippling anxiety, the intense self-loathing, the erasure of memory and unfocused concentration, and the "dank joylessness like some poisonous fog-bank rolling in." Eschewing psychoactive drugs and therapy, Styron writes that for him the real healers were time and seclusion. This conclusion is supported by many of the people I interviewed who were asked to describe how they came to terms with their most difficult time during their twenties. Basically, they toughed it out.

Styron asserts that depression is a kind of biochemical meltdown that affects the brain as well as the mind. He feels it is as serious and as life-threatening as diabetes or cancer.

☐ **Ten Ways to Stay Sane**
- Make a lot of friends
- Make a point of getting along with your family, boss, and colleagues
- Three days a week, spend three hours doing whatever you want
- Steer clear of drugs and excessive alcohol
- Do something fun for exercise
- Recognize your trouble spots — what stresses you out?
- Ask for help when you need it
- Find a good therapist
- Life is too short to be in unhealthy relationships
- Keep a journal

Those who have never experienced it will seldom understand the force of its physical anguish. There are still a lot of public misconceptions about depression. For more on this, see Styron's moving book *Darkness Visible: A Memoir of Madness.*

Afterword

LIFE's transitions are too uneven, messy, and unpredictable to be addressed using simplistic formulas. This is why so many self-help books wind up being "shelf"-help. Take what you find useful in this book and discard the rest. Although prospering through this period in your life will at times require courage and hard work, I believe that paying attention to these issues will help you to survive, and may even sharpen your focus. I myself will be rereading this book in the knowledge that we teach what we most need to learn.

I have a lot of hope for our generation. We are thinking more and rushing less. We are growing up before we have families. We are questioning the wisdom of a workaholic lifestyle and cow-like consumption patterns. We are travelling and learning about other nations. This is all good, solid stuff from my point of view. The issues facing us today are too serious for us to live our lives irresponsibly. Although there are contradictions inherent in our aspirations to raise decent kids and still succeed in our careers, we are in a position to see the fallout from previous generations' experiences and adjust our approaches accordingly. We are waiting, and though perhaps we have not yet made all the commitments our lives will require of us, at least we are not swallowing the traditional formulas unthinkingly. In my interviews I sensed a sophistication and an irreverent wisdom about these topics that was exciting to share.

I hope I have given voice to some of the issues on which our culture is often all too silent. I am most concerned that we all be more aware of the value of friendship and need for relationship skills, that we understand how to go about exploring the different options life makes available to us, and that we learn how to cultivate the skills that will help us chart our way out of confusion. These are the greatest sources of turmoil in our twenties. How do you navigate a love relationship fraught with emotional danger? How do you go about finding work when you're not at all sure where to begin? How do you build a career after that? The first step is taken by starting from where you are, and not from where you think you should be. The second step is taken by keeping in mind that you participate in the construction of your own life moment by moment. You have more control than you may realize.

STEVEN GIBB is 27 and lives in Ann Arbor, Michigan. After spending part of his youth in Chile and Peru, he went on to attend the Residential College at the University of Michigan, the University of Sussex (U.K.), and Purdue University, where he will be receiving a master's degree in marriage and family therapy. This is his first book.